What Your Colleagues Are Saying . . .

Jackie Walsh has written a must-read book for administrators and teachers who are considering best practices to invest in students' ability to excel in their own questioning. Read this book and learn from one of the best.

—Lisa Berry
Assistant Superintendent for Curriculum and Instruction
Trussville City Schools, AL

Jackie Walsh leaves no stone unturned in her journey to share proven questioning strategies gleaned from years of field experience and partnerships with teachers. She offers readers a unique categorization of student questions that provides a framework and common vocabulary for building a culture of questioning. Not only does this book offer turnkey tools, protocols, and routines for educators to increase questioning practices, it also provides metacognitive processes and reflection guides for student use. It's a must-have for educators on a mission to empower students with the knowledge and disposition of questioning.

—Jana Claxton
Professional Learning Coordinator
Irving ISD, TX

I have a question: Why don't you have this book? It's filled with amazing ideas that encourage students to ask questions. In doing so, you will spark students' curiosity and wonder. You will capture their minds and hearts and, I promise, they will learn more.

—Douglas Fisher
Professor of Educational Leadership
San Diego State University

Empowered students become leaders of their own learning, resulting in success in school, career, and life. In her latest book, Empowering Students as Questioners, *Jackie Walsh provides a formula to empower students through questioning. I particularly appreciate the actionable steps to help students self-question so they can monitor their progress, deepen their understanding, and discover new ideas and concepts to explore. This book is filled with resources, including videos of practitioners who have honed their craft by engaging students as questioners. Teachers will refer to it time and time again as they seek to support their students in deep and meaningful learning.*

—Cathy W. Gassenheimer
Executive Vice President
Alabama Best Practices Center

Any teacher who seeks to unleash student curiosity should have this book on their shelf, underlined, dog-eared, and full of margin notes. We've long known (yet often neglected) the power of curiosity to fuel student learning. The real "magic" of curiosity happens, of course, when students begin to ask their questions. For many teachers, though, getting students who barely respond to teacher questions to ask their own questions may feel like a bridge too far. With compelling insights and practical strategies, Jackie Walsh shows teachers how to get from here to there, creating classrooms where students take charge of their own learning by asking themselves questions to reflect on their progress, deepen their understanding, and unleash their curiosity so they become lifelong learners.

—Bryan Goodwin
President and CEO, McREL International
Author, *Building a Curious School*

Empowering students to become skillful and confident in constructing and asking questions is making a positive impact on the overall instructional climate of classrooms across my district. I observe teachers transforming the student role from that of occasional responder to teacher questions to one of actively engaged questioner. This change is resulting from the commitment of classroom teachers and instructional leaders at all levels in our district. In Jackie Walsh's new book, you'll find classroom examples illustrating the skills, strategies, and structures that support students in becoming more engaged in and responsible for their learning.

—Jeff Goodwin
Superintendent of Oxford City Schools
Alabama Superintendent of the Year, 2020

Jackie Walsh invites us to explore the teacher mindframe, "I am intentional in nurturing students as questioners." So how can we create classroom cultures that welcome authentic questions and make a real impact on student learning? Questions are the essence of curiosity and they invite a sense of wonder, which is a great invitation to learning, the beginning of problem-solving, and the best prompt to motivate inquiring and understanding. There is no question, this is the right book to answer this challenge.

—John Hattie
Laureate Professor, Melbourne Graduate School of Education
Co-author, *The Distance Learning Playbook*

Giving students the ability and opportunity to question not only academic content, but also the world they live in, is an invaluable skill that will benefit them throughout their lives. This book provides clear, common-sense strategies that can be embedded in any curriculum to impact learning for ALL students. It will be a vital resource for me as

I work with teachers across my campus to improve engagement, instruction, and success for students.

—Sarah Menn
Instructional Coach, Byron Nelson High School
Trophy Club, TX

Empowering Students as Questioners *is the perfect balance of merging theory and practice. After making a powerful case for the why, Jackie Walsh provides structures and tools for equipping teachers to bring out the inquisitive nature and curiosity that exist within their students. If you have a desire to empower students to engage in meaningful inquiry, reflection, analysis, and discourse, then this is the book for you!*

—Jamie Parris
Director of High School Teaching and Learning
Hamilton County Schools, TN

"Student questions are strong levers for learning." Jackie Walsh once again successfully reminds educators of the value of using questions for both student growth and sound instructional decision-making during the learning process. Whether through self-questioning, personal reflection, exploratory questioning, or dialogical questioning, the reader will be challenged to contemplate how the process of using think time and other modes of questioning ignites the potential for learning in any classroom for both students and the classroom practitioner.

—Bradley A. Scott
Instructional Leader
Huntsville, AL

Rigor occurs when learners have their own thoughts about unique, original, or new content and strategy and when they are engaged enough to persevere. Empowering Students as Questioners *provides educators a gateway for designing engaging and rigorous learning experiences for students. Jackie Walsh is masterful at explaining how to use strategies and structures to develop students as questioners who are seeking to become self-regulated learners striving to make meaning of the world around them. I love this book, from the opening powerful task design in Ms. Shelton's ninth-grade classroom, to explicitly teaching students how to assume the role of questioners versus answerers of teacher questions. It is a must-read for those who are committed to transforming classroom spaces where not knowing an answer is viewed as an opportunity to learn rather than a sign of failure.*

—Terri Stice
Consultant and author, *Powerful Task Design*
Bowling Green, KY

"Asking the right question at the right time is one of the most powerful skills to acquire. It's a nuanced art that can always be refined and augmented. Whether you are a beginning teacher or a veteran, this book is just what you need to grow your students' confidence and competence as questioners in the classroom. Regardless of the grade or subject matter you teach, Jackie Acree Walsh has written this book for you. She combines practical advice and accessible research to encourage thoughtful questioning that engages learners and adds energy to your classroom."

—**Sarah Brown Wessling**
NBCT 2010 National Teacher of the Year
Johnston, IA

Empowering Students as Questioners

Empowering Students as Questioners

Skills, Strategies, and Structures to Realize the Potential of Every Learner

Jackie Acree Walsh

Foreword by Jim Knight

FOR INFORMATION:

Corwin

A SAGE Company

2455 Teller Road

Thousand Oaks, California 91320

(800) 233-9936

www.corwin.com

SAGE Publications Ltd.

1 Oliver's Yard

55 City Road

London EC1Y 1SP

United Kingdom

SAGE Publications India Pvt. Ltd.

B 1/I 1 Mohan Cooperative Industrial Area

Mathura Road, New Delhi 110 044

India

SAGE Publications Asia-Pacific Pte. Ltd.

18 Cross Street #10-10/11/12

China Square Central

Singapore 048423

Publisher: Jessica Allan

Senior Content
    Development Editor: Lucas Schleicher

Associate Content
    Development Editor: Mia Rodriguez

Project Editor: Amy Schroller

Copy Editor: Karin Rathert

Typesetter: C&M Digitals (P) Ltd.

Proofreader: Lawrence W. Baker

Indexer: Integra

Cover Designer: Candice Harman

Printed in the United States of America

Library of Congress Cataloging-in-Publication Data

Names: Walsh, Jackie A., author.

Title: Empowering students as questioners : skills, strategies, and structures to realize the potential of every learner / Jackie Acree Walsh.

Description: Thousand Oaks, California : Corwin, [2021] | Includes bibliographical references and index.

Identifiers: LCCN 2020042515 | ISBN 9781544331744 (paperback) | ISBN 9781544331751 (epub) | ISBN 9781544331768 (epub) | ISBN 9781544331782 (pdf)

Subjects: LCSH: Inquiry-based learning. | Questioning. | Teacher-student relationships.

Classification: LCC LB1027.23 .W38 2021 | DDC 371.3—dc23

LC record available at https://lccn.loc.gov/2020042515

This book is printed on acid-free paper.

21 22 23 24 25 10 9 8 7 6 5 4 3 2 1

Contents

LIST OF FIGURES   xi

LIST OF VIDEOS   xiii

FOREWORD   xv
  Jim Knight

ACKNOWLEDGMENTS   xvii

ABOUT THE AUTHOR   xix

CHAPTER 1 STUDENT QUESTIONING—TRANSFORMING
     LEARNING FOR ALL   1

  Why Is Student Question-Asking Important? *Making the Case*   2

  Why Should Teachers Incorporate Student Questions
    Into Their Instruction? *Filling a Void*   6

  What Propels Student Questioners? *The Skill, the Will, and the Thrill*   7

  How Can We Develop Students' Skill and Will to Ask Questions
    in Class? *About This Book*   15

CHAPTER 2 TEACHERS AS ACTIVATORS—COMMITTING
     TO CHANGE, CREATING THE CULTURE   19

  How Can Teachers Motivate Students? *Creating the Classroom Culture*   20

  How Should Teachers Proceed? *Setting Explicit Expectations*   22

  How Can Teachers Transform Learning? *A Process to Build Capacity*   24

CHAPTER 3 SELF-QUESTIONS—MONITORING LEARNING
     AND MAKING MEANING   37

  Monitoring Learning—*Developing Student Capacity to
    Ask Questions to Self-Regulate*   39

  Making Meaning—*Developing Student Capacity to Ask
    Self-Questions to Build Understanding*   52

CHAPTER 4 ACADEMIC QUESTIONS—CLARIFYING AND
DEEPENING UNDERSTANDING   61

Building a Knowledge Base—*Developing Student Capacity
  to Ask Academic Questions*   63

CHAPTER 5 EXPLORATORY QUESTIONS—EXPRESSING
WONDERINGS AND CURIOSITIES   79

Nurturing Curiosity—*Developing Student Capacity to
  Ask Exploratory Questions*   82

CHAPTER 6 DIALOGIC QUESTIONS—CLARIFYING AND
DEEPENING UNDERSTANDING   99

Broadening Perspectives—*Developing Student Capacity to
  Ask Dialogic Questions*   101

CHAPTER 7 THE END IN MIND—INCREASED AGENCY
WITHIN AND BEYOND THE CLASSROOM   123

Beyond Scaffolding—*Toward a Holistic Approach*   125
Realizing the Potential—*In School and Beyond*   128

REFERENCES   131

INDEX   137

List of Figures

NUMBER	TITLE	PAGE
Figure 1.1	Taxonomy of Student Questions	9
Figure 1.2	Think Time 1 Poster	12
Figure 1.3	Think Time 2 Poster	12
Figure 2.1a	Informal Inventory of Student Question-Asking	25
Figure 2.1b	Student Survey	26
Figure 2.2	A Process to Build Capacity	27
Figure 3.1	Cycle of Student Self-Questioning to Learn*	41
Figure 3.2	Self-Questioning Skills for Self-Regulation	44
Figure 3.3	Generic Prompts for Use in Activating Student Questions at Different Stages of Learning	47
Figure 3.4	Self-Questioning Skills for Use During Silent Reading or Listening	54
Figure 3.5	Prompts and Stems for Use Before, During, and After Reading	54
Figure 3.6	Prompts for Student Self-Questions in Mathematical Problem-Solving	56
Figure 4.1	Skills and Stems to Support Surface Learning	65
Figure 4.2	Skills and Stems to Support Deep Learning	66
Figure 4.3	Skills and Stems to Support Transfer Learning	67
Figure 4.4	Criteria for a Student-Created Academic Question	67
Figure 4.5	Praise-Question-Polish	73
Figure 5.1	Skills and Sample Prompts Associated With Exploratory Questions	85
Figure 5.2	Criteria for Exploratory Questions	92
Figure 6.1	Sample Prompt and Stems for Dialogic Questions	103
Figure 6.2	Three Categories of Dialogic Questions	104

(Continued)

(Continued)

NUMBER	TITLE	PAGE
Figure 6.3	Criteria for a Quality Dialogic Question	105
Figure 7.1	Types of Questions	125
Figure 7.2	Process for Developing Student Capacity as Questioners	125

List of Videos

Note From the Publisher: The author has provided access to video content throughout the book that is available to you through QR codes. To read a QR code, you must have a smartphone or tablet with a camera. We recommend that you download a QR code reader app that is made specifically for your phone or tablet brand.

NUMBER	TITLE	PAGE
Video 1.1	**Why Do Student Questions? Eighth Graders' Perspectives** *Focus Group of Eighth Graders*	2
Video 1.2	**Leaders Tout Benefits of Students as Questioners** *Oxford, AL, City Schools, Superintendent Jeff Goodwin and Principals Heath Harmon, Christy Shepard, and Amy Copeland*	5
Video 1.3	**Think Times: Key Building Blocks for Culture** *Jordan Whaley and Lori Woodrow, Sixth Grade*	14
Video 2.1	**Collaborative Planning for Student Questions** *Oxford High School Biology Team*	20
Video 2.2	**What Makes a Question a Quality One?** *Brittany Pinkard, Fourth Grade*	24
Video 2.3	**How Can Questioning Skills Be Woven Into Daily Learning Targets?** *K-12 Teachers in Oxford City Schools*	29
Video 2.4	**Peer Feedback for Student Questions** *Tracy Ray, Third Grade*	31
Video 3.1	**The Value of Questions in Design Thinking** *Oxford High School Green Car Team*	38
Video 3.2	**Self-Questioning to Monitor Reading Comprehension** *Jennifer Patterson, Second Grade*	55
Video 4.1	**Student Questions Propel Learning of Geometry** *Jarid Moore, Geometry*	62

(Continued)

(Continued)

NUMBER	TITLE	PAGE
Video 4.2	**Student Questions Drive Learning in U.S. History** *Adam Clark, Eleventh-Grade U.S. History*	70
Video 4.3	**Peer Feedback Using Praise-Question-Polish** *Cade Somers, Tenth-Grade English*	72
Video 5.1	**Stimulating Curiosity and Exploratory Questions in a Biology Class** *Meredith Barkley, High School Biology*	80
Video 5.2	**Collaborative Generation of Exploratory Questions** *Kehaulani Bohannon, First Grade*	86
Video 5.3	**Activating Sixth Graders' Curiosity About Historical Issues** *Stephanie Hendrix, Sixth Grade*	89
Video 6.1	**Asking Questions to Understand Different Perspectives** *Lauren Phifer, Ninth-Grade World History, and* *Michelle Shelton, Ninth-Grade English*	100
Video 6.2	**Dialogic Questions and Design Thinking** *Krista Mintz, Mathematics and Computer Science, and* *Britton Young, Biology*	104
Video 6.3	**Dialogic Questioning Using Interview Design** *Michelle Shelton, Ninth-Grade English*	113
Video 7.1	**Teachers Dialogue About Power of Student Questions** *Krista Mintz, Mathematics and Computer Science, and* *Britton Young, Biology*	124
Video 7.2	**Students Relate Their Future Success to the Ability to Ask Questions** *Eighth-Grade Focus Group*	129

EMPOWERING STUDENTS AS QUESTIONERS

Foreword

I am grateful for the chance to say a few words about this wonderful book. Writing this foreword gives me a chance to say thank you to the book's author, Jackie Walsh. I have spent my professional life studying and popularizing coaching. Questions are a central part of coaching, and Jackie's work has had a huge impact on how I ask questions. In my professional universe, Jackie is a big star.

I am also grateful for the chance to write about this book because I believe it is one that especially needs to be read right now. As I write this in November 2020, we are seeing the most tumultuous time that I've experienced in my 65 years on earth. Some of the change is very healthy and long past due. In the United States and around the world, we are seeing an awakening to systemic racism, and many people are realizing that structures must change to ensure we live in an equitable society.

Other changes we're experiencing are not as healthy. COVID-19 has turned our world upside down. People are worried that they or their loved ones might get a deadly disease and about whether or not they will have a job. Educators and many others don't know what their job will look like week by week. On top of these changes, we are currently led by a president whose divide-and-conquer approach to leadership has polarized the United States.

These are challenging and uncertain times, and I am reminded of one of my favorite quotations from Eric Hoffer: "In times of change, the learners inherit the earth, and the learned find themselves beautifully equipped for a world that no longer exists." To make the best of what we are experiencing, we need to be learners. And, of course, to be learners, we need to ask good questions. What's more, the people who most need to learn questioning skills are those who will shape our future society: our children. That is why I am so grateful for this book.

Jackie Walsh offers educators a frame for thinking about and teaching students four types of questions: self-questions, academic questions, exploratory questions, and dialogic questions. All four are important for student academic success because they prepare our young people to achieve success beyond school—to achieve their personal potential and work with others to create new structures and norms for the fragmented world they will inherit.

Self-questions facilitate personal reflection leading to self-regulation. Academic questions enable learners to move from surface knowledge to deep understanding.

Exploratory questions encourage curiosity and creativity. And, my personal favorite, dialogic questions open the door to better conversations out of which can emerge the collaborative solutions needed to address seemingly insurmountable problems.

A central theme in the book is that empowering students as questioners acknowledges them as equal partners in the teaching-learning equation. Providing learners with voice and choice through questioning leads them to own their learning. Using questions to enhance reflection and dialogue contributes to personal and collective responsibility for learning. All of these result in reciprocity in a community where teacher and students are questioning, listening, and learning with and from one another. I believe that students who practice these principles in school will adopt them as a way of interacting with others in their futures.

To close, let me provide two questions for you to think about as you read this book:

Do you think it's important that our children become more proficient in asking questions?

How will you use the ideas in this book to empower students to be better questioners?

—Jim Knight, PhD
Research Associate, University of Kansas
Senior Partner, Instructional Coaching Group
Lawrence, KS

Acknowledgments

Insight and inspiration are essential to authoring a book. This is especially true for this book, which has been a labor of love. I learned the value of student questions from my own children, from students whom I taught, and from countless teachers with whom I've worked.

Important insights emerged as I watched my children, Catherine and Will, develop and mature as questioners and learners from their earliest years. Many of their teachers welcomed their questions; some did not. I wondered why this was the case, and so my journey began. They and my granddaughters, Bea and Taylor, continue to inspire me to learn more about the why and how of student questioning.

Over many years, I've been privileged to work with thousands of teachers committed to improving classroom questioning. Many have asked, *Why don't students ask more questions? How can we encourage our students to ask questions, not just answer them?* Their comments and questions inspired me to search for answers.

In 2019, Khristie Goodwin, Coordinator of Curriculum and Instructional Programs, in Oxford (AL) City Schools, invited me to lead professional learning in quality questioning for all teachers in this district. Leaders and teachers in Oxford became my partners in learning more about student questioning. Fourteen of these teachers, featured in vignettes and videos throughout this book, committed to the deep work of collaborating with their students and one another to develop the skills and mindframes featured in the pages that follow. Their classrooms became laboratories in which they and their students learned to use strategies and structures to build student skills as questioners. And the results were phenomenal! Students did develop, in the words of Ron Berger (2014), as *leaders of their own learning*. Without the commitment, courage, and hard work of these teachers and students, this book might never have come to fruition.

Beth Sattes, my long-time friend, colleague, and coauthor, provided invaluable insights before and during my writing of this book. For many years, Beth and I reflected on the importance of student questions as we worked with teachers across the United States to integrate quality questioning into their practice. While personal considerations prevented Beth from coauthoring this round, she was an important thought partner throughout.

Jessica Allan's belief in this project has been unwavering. As my Corwin editor, Jessica encouraged me over the years of its incubation and final emergence. Her understanding and patience inspired me to continue this work after a number of unforeseen interruptions. Her keen insights made this book better.

Finally, in 2020, the year of COVID-19, I acknowledge the professionalism, ingenuity, flexibility, and incredible hard work of teachers everywhere and at all levels of education. Your commitment to your students during these challenging times inspires me and makes me even more proud to be a member of this amazing profession.

Jackie A. Walsh
Montgomery, AL
August 14, 2020

About the Author

Jackie Acree Walsh is an independent consultant who partners with educators across the country to enhance teaching and leading. Her passion and primary area of expertise is questioning—to advance both student and adult learning. Based in Montgomery, Alabama, Jackie is the lead consultant for the Alabama Best Practices Center, which affords her the opportunity to design learning over time for members of statewide networks. Her career spans work in K–12, higher education, state agencies, and research laboratories.

Jackie's early experience as a high school social studies teacher contributed to her lifelong interest in classroom questioning. She designs professional learning that focuses on changing classroom questioning practices and uses feedback from teachers and leaders to customize resources and learning experiences to local contexts. Decades of observing and listening to teachers have contributed to Jackie's evolving understanding of how teachers can work with students to change patterns of engagement and increase learning through questioning.

The author and coauthor of numerous books and articles focused on quality questioning, Jackie seeks to make research and best practice accessible to practitioners. Her books, coauthored with Beth Sattes, include *Quality Questioning*, 2nd edition (2017), *Questioning for Classroom Discussion* (2015), *Thinking Through Quality Questioning* (2011), and *Leading Through Quality Questioning* (2010). She received her AB from Duke University, MAT from the University of North Carolina (Chapel Hill), and PhD from the University of Alabama.

Follow Jackie on Twitter @Question2Think; email, walshja@aol.com.

To teachers everywhere who responded to the challenges of 2020 with courage and grace

CHAPTER 1

Student Questioning

Transforming Learning for All

Student Questioners at Work

A focus group of eighth-grade students dialogue about the value of student questions for learning in school. As they reflect on opportunities to form and ask questions in class, they agree that too often teachers don't provide adequate time for students to think of and ask their own questions. These young people also agree that asking and answering questions with peers deepens their understanding and broadens their thinking. Video 1.1 features their dialogue about the ways in which the opportunity to form their own questions supports their learning. ▪

Video 1.1: "Why Do Student Questions? Eighth Graders' Perspectives"

Student questions motivate, firing young imaginations. Student questions engage, moving learners to wonder about their world. Student questions lead to answers, enabling the questioners to build a storehouse of knowledge. *All* students have questions, which can empower them to be successful learners. Ritchhart and Church (2020) maintain that "Questions not only drive thinking and learning, they are also outcomes of it" (p. 25). Why, then, are student questions so uncommon in classrooms? Why do so many students, particularly low-performing students, refrain from ever asking?

These questions are the inspiration behind each page of this book. Student questions can enhance outcomes for *all* learners. Student questions can serve to engage underachievers. Student questions can level the playing field and close the achievement gap. Developing students as questioners is a worthy goal for all teachers.

WHY IS STUDENT QUESTION-ASKING IMPORTANT? MAKING THE CASE

Student questions are strong levers for learning—for both students and teachers. The strongest arguments for focusing more time and attention on students as questioners come directly from students and teachers.

STUDENTS TAKE OWNERSHIP OF THEIR LEARNING

In Michelle Shelton's ninth-grade English class, students are working in collaborative teams creating questions to explore how the trial in *To Kill a Mockingbird* might have differed had it occurred in other specified time periods. A productive buzz permeates the classroom. When asked about the value of forming their own questions, students respond: "I care much more about my questions [than I do about my teacher's]." "When I talk with my group members to develop a question, I learn a lot from them." "When I think of questions that Scout might have asked, I start to better understand her character."

> "Just as asking precedes answering in the questioning process, so do student questions come before teacher questions in the learning process. For when students ask, learning follows."—J. T. Dillon, *Questioning and Teaching: A Manual of Practice*, p. 7

Beyond this anecdotal evidence is an impressive body of research and theory. First, consider the overriding themes related to benefits for students.

1. *Student motivation and ownership of their learning increase.* A review of experimental evidence spanning five decades supports the notion that "children's intrinsic interest is the most powerful ingredient in learning" (S. Engel, 2015). Student questions are strong catalysts for releasing this intrinsic interest (W. Berger & Foster, 2020; Perkins, 1992; Wells, 2001). In short, students are more cognitively, emotionally, and socially engaged in learning when provided the opportunity to ask questions.

2. *Students are better able to monitor their progress toward identified learning outcomes.* Student questions support self-regulation, reflection, and monitoring of their learning, a key element of metacognitive thinking. When students are actively engaged in reflecting on their learning, they are better able to understand and retain complex concepts (Ostroff, 2012).

3. *Student performance on academic tasks improves.* Research focusing on the relationship between student questions and achievement outcomes spans kindergarten through higher education and all content areas. Opportunities for students to form and ask questions to themselves, their classmates, and their teachers are consistently linked to higher levels of performance (Berry & Chew, 2008; Dillon, 1988; Hunkins, 1995; Oakes & Lipton, 1999).

4. *Students are better prepared for the next levels of education.* A seminal study of the knowledge and skills required for college success (Conley, 2005) found students' habits of mind to be as important as prior content knowledge. Among the most important are "critical thinking, analytic thinking, problem solving; an inquisitive nature . . . ; openness to possible failures . . . ; and ability and desire to cope with frustrating and ambiguous learning tasks" (p. 173). Student ability and willingness to ask questions are core skills running through all of these habits of mind.

5. *Students are better prepared for the workplace.* Wagner and Dintersmith (2015) make a strong case for the importance of question-asking to success on the job,

> "We are going to need questioning leaders to move the world forward. I'm referring to not just top corporate executives but team leaders of any type, as well as civic leaders, social advocates, "thought leaders," family leaders, and, of course, educators."
> (W. Berger & Foster, 2020, p. 19)

joining a host of thought leaders who advocate for questioning as an essential 21st century skill (Partnership for 21st Century Learning, 2019; W. Berger, 2018; W. Berger & Foster, 2020; Minigan, 2017). Minigan (2017), for example, argues that curiosity and question formation are key to success in today's world, both complementing the four Cs associated with the Framework for 21st Century Learning—creativity, critical thinking, communication, and collaboration—and as ends in and of themselves.

6. *Students are better able to assume civic responsibilities.* John Dewey viewed public education as a prerequisite to effective functioning of democratic societies. He argued that the ability to inquire into problems, to question, was essential to productive citizenship (Turnbull, 2004). More recently, Schlesinger (2009) argues that the survival of democratic institutions depends on its citizenry's ability to ask questions. In *The Death of Why?: The Decline of Questioning and the Future of Democracy*, this author laments our current-day obsession with answers and calls for a renewed belief in the value and power of questions.

SCHOOL LEADERS AFFIRM THE VALUE OF STUDENTS AS QUESTIONERS

A primary responsibility of educational leaders is to involve their communities in creating a vision for teaching and learning that will empower today's students to succeed in the ever-changing future they are facing. Michael Fullan has long advocated for innovation and reform within school systems. In *Deep Learning* (Fullan & McEachen, 2018), he addresses two issues challenging the relevance of traditional schooling: (1) the disengagement of students who are not responding to teacher-centered instruction, and (2) the unpredictable and declining job market driven, at least in part, by the rise of robots (p. 3). Fullan and colleagues offer a vision for learning that is grounded in inquiry and increases student ownership, both of which are advanced by student questions.

Questioners at Work

School administrators within Oxford (AL) City Schools have been instrumental in nurturing and supporting shifts in classroom practice that empower students to become "leaders of their own learning" (R. Berger, 2014). The superintendent leads the way in envisioning learning experiences that equip all students across this diverse community for success in their changing environment. He and, K-12 school leaders offer the vision and support to teachers who are adapting the skills, strategies, and structures offered in this book to meet the needs of their students and to empower these young people as questioners. Listen to Superintendent Jeff Goodwin and three of his principals speak to the why of students as questioners. ∎

Video 1.2: "Leaders Tout Benefits of Students as Questioners."

TEACHERS LEARN WHERE THEIR STUDENTS ARE IN THEIR LEARNING

Jarid Moore, eighth-grade geometry teacher, often ends class by asking each student to formulate the question they need to answer to take the next step in learning. These questions serve as their exit tickets. Mr. Moore reflects, "In this class, the questions usually fall into three categories: (1) those indicating confusion about a basic concept, (2) those suggesting a need for more practice, and (3) those that go way beyond mastery of the standard—sometimes into areas that I've never thought about. I use their questions as formative feedback to help me structure the next day's lesson."

Research affirms Mr. Moore's claim that student questions represent authentic feedback informing teachers of where a student is in a learning progression (J. Engel, 1988; S. Engel, 2015; Ritchhart & Church, 2020). This feedback enables differentiation, the provision of "just-right" support to individual students, and assists in proper pacing of lessons for the whole group.

Student questions support effective teaching and learning in a myriad of ways. Among other arguments for increasing student questions are the following:

1. *Student questions serve to clarify misunderstandings for their peers.* When one student raises a question, other students who may have been similarly confused benefit. The listening students may not have known exactly how to put their confusion into words, but they experience ahas as the questioner's wondering is addressed (J. Engel, 1988).

2. *Student questions can help close achievement gaps occasioned by cultural, language, and/or learning differences.* Fast-paced, teacher-centered instruction "works" for most mainstream, middle-class students. Many English language learners,

students with learning disabilities, and students who are economically disadvantaged are not always able to make immediate meaning of the explanations provided by textbooks and teachers. When students learn how to frame questions and are provided structured opportunities to reflect and identify their own "needs to know," they become more engaged. As a result, their understanding of content and subsequent performance improves (Berkeley et al., 2010; Matibag-Angeles, 2016; Ostroff, 2016). Students from minority cultural and ethnic groups can reap similar benefits when invited to generate their wonderings and "needs to know."

3. *Teachers have fewer interruptions from disengaged students*. When students are actively engaged in thinking about and forming their questions and in asking and responding to questions with their peers, they are intrinsically motivated. Students who regularly "act out" now focus on learning, not on attention-seeking or distracting others.

Time and again, students who are empowered as questioners echo the refrain of Mrs. Shelton's students: *"We like it when our teacher provides time for us to create and ask our questions. We are more engaged, and we learn more."* Likewise, almost all teachers working to develop students as questioners repeat Mr. Moore's claim: *"Student questions provide me with some of the best formative feedback I receive."* These two reasons provide a sufficient justification for placing increased emphasis on students as questioners. They address important levers for student achievement.

Why Should Teachers Incorporate Student Questions Into Their Instruction? Filling a Void

Given the many benefits of student question-asking in school, one might think it a widespread occurrence. The opposite is the case. Classroom research over many decades consistently reports a dearth of student questions across all grade levels and content areas (Barnett et al., 1995; Dillon, 1988; S. Engel, 2015; Hunkins, 1995; Rowe, 1972).

The low incidence of student questions in science classes prompted science educator Mary Budd Rowe to initiate research leading to the "discovery of wait times." Rowe focused her early research (1972) on elementary science classrooms. Over a five-year period, she examined 300 classrooms and found only three in which students were engaged in asking questions. In these three classrooms, teachers were pausing following the asking of questions and after student responses. Rowe concluded that an increase in student questions is one of the benefits of consistent use of wait times.

Dillon (1988), a long-time student of classroom questioning, summarized data from his observations of dozens of classrooms:

> "Questions accounted for over 60 per cent of the teachers' talk and for less than one per cent of the students' talk. The overall rate works out to 80 questions per hour from each teacher and two questions per hour from all the students combined." (p. 9)

Dillon determined that students in the observed classrooms did not possess question-asking skills and focused his work on the development of procedures and processes to enhance student ability in this area.

When asked, teachers confirm the finding of research: Very few students ask substantive questions during class. In my and Beth Sattes's work in facilitating professional learning on questioning, we've collected responses from hundreds of teachers related to classroom questioning. These teachers responded individually to this question through participation in the Interview Design protocol: *Research reports that students ask less than 5 percent of the questions in both elementary and secondary classrooms. Why do students initiate so few questions? Offer three or four hypotheses.* Five responses appeared time and again:

- The fast pace of most classrooms doesn't allow time for questions.
- Students are afraid of being embarrassed.
- Students don't know how or don't feel comfortable asking.
- Classrooms are teacher driven, not student centered.
- The teacher is the expert; it is the teacher's role to question.

(Walsh & Sattes, 2015)

Of particular interest is the widespread teacher belief that "students don't know how or don't feel comfortable." A primary goal of this book is to provide strategies and tools teachers can use to increase students' knowledge of how to form questions and their comfort level in asking.

WHAT PROPELS STUDENT QUESTIONERS? THE SKILL, THE WILL, AND THE THRILL

Hattie and Donoghue (2016) use *skill*, *will*, and *thrill* to represent three primary inputs and outputs in their Model of Learning. *Skill* relates to knowledge and skills; *will* embodies the "dispositions . . . habits of mind or tendencies to respond to situations in a certain way"; and *thrill* conveys "the motivational aspects of learning" (p. 2). While this model of learning is not centered on building the capacity of students as questioners, *skill, will,* and *thrill* do inspire three questions to guide the reader's reflection and response throughout the book.

- *What knowledge and* **skills** *do my students need to be effective questioners?*

- *How can I help my students develop the* **will**, *the frames of mind, to form and ask questions to advance their learning?*

- *How can I partner with my students in developing a classroom culture where they can experience the* **thrill** *of learning by asking and answering their own questions?*

SKILL: DEVELOPING KNOWLEDGE OF QUESTION TYPES

If students are to assume the role of questioners, they need to know the features and functions of questions that support learning. A small percentage of students arrive at school with tacit knowledge of different kinds and purposes of questions. Most do not. Teaching students about the forms and purposes of questions is requisite to developing their skills in question-asking. In the following chapter, you will have an opportunity to reflect on how to proceed in integrating student learning about questions into daily lessons.

> Teaching students about the forms and purposes of questions is requisite to developing their skills in question-asking.

Student questions serve a variety of purposes in school and real-life settings. Questions that support student learning in classrooms fall into four categories—self-questions, academic questions, exploratory questions, and dialogic questions. These four compose the Taxonomy of Student Questions presented as Figure 1.1. Students infrequently ask these four types of questions. Almost all of the questions they do ask in class are procedural in nature, posed to clarify directions (e.g., *What page did you ask us to turn turn?*), make a personal request (e.g., *May I sharpen my pencil?"),* or find out about a nonacademic matter (e.g., *What's for lunch? When will we get our test back?*) (Dillon, 1988, p. 10; S. Engel, 2015, p. 12). Each of the four question types comprising the Taxonomy advance understanding and performance.

The components of the Taxonomy do not have a hierarchical relationship to one another. They serve different purposes while working together to advance student learning. All questions initially form within a learner's mind in response to external stimuli. Self-questions are those that learners answer for themselves. Supporting individual metacognitive and meaning-making processes, self-questions may never surface publicly. Academic questions assist the learner in developing understandings related to the topic under study, in making progress toward identified

FIGURE 1.1   Taxonomy of Student Questions

learning goals. Exploratory questions stem from curiosity. A fourth category, dialogic questions, arises out of a need to get behind another's thinking, to understand a different point of view. Academic, exploratory, and dialogic questions are most frequently posed to others to elicit responses that provide information or insights to the questioner.

WILL: NURTURING QUESTIONING MINDFRAMES

How can teachers encourage students to assume a new role in classrooms—that of questioners, not solely answerers of teacher questions? Beyond equipping them with knowledge and skills and providing time and a safe space for their questions, teachers can help students develop a personal *why*, help them understand what's in it for them. For many students, this involves developing new attitudes or outlooks related to their competence and confidence in question-asking. Such attitudes impact a student's *self-efficacy*, "the belief in one's ability to take action, accomplish a task, and reach goals" (Bandura, 2011). Self-efficacy has a high effect size ($d = 0.90$) or impact on student achievement (Hattie & Donoghue, 2016, p. 5). Fostering student self-efficacy with regard to the asking of questions is key to actualizing this process in the classroom. The attitudes or outlooks required by students are questioning mindframes.

> Fostering student self-efficacy with regard to the asking of questions is key to actualizing this process in the classroom.

The student questioning mindframes relate to question types, two for self-questions and one for each of the other three. As students begin understanding and embracing these, their will to ask questions is strengthened. Anchor charts or posters can serve as daily reminders of these responsibilities of questioners.

Notice that each mindframe is formulated as a positive, empowering statement of commitment to the purpose behind the particular question type. The expectation is that students will adopt these ways of thinking and manifest them in routine classroom behaviors. Specific mindframes are associated with each question type.

- Self-Questions—Metacognitive: *I ask questions to myself to monitor my thinking and learning.*

- Self-Questions—Cognitive: *I ask questions to figure out the meaning of what I am reading or hearing and to think through problems and tasks.*

- Academic Questions: *I pose questions to clarify and deepen my understanding of academic content.*

- Exploratory Questions: *I use questions to channel my curiosity and spark my creativity.*

- Dialogic Questions: *I use questions to understand other perspectives and to engage in collaborative thinking and learning.*

THRILL: CO-CREATING A QUESTIONING CULTURE

A primary deterrent to student questions is the fear that asking may either reveal ignorance or expose one as an overzealous learner. These fears relate to social-emotional factors and vary by age and peer-group affiliation. Self-confident learners who possess a strong sense of identity and agency are less likely to have such fears. Consider the words of poet e. e. cummings: "once we believe in ourselves, we can risk curiosity, wonder, spontaneous delight, or any experience that reveals the human spirit" (cited in Frey, Fisher, & Smith, 2019). Curiosity, wonder, spontaneous delight. How beautifully these words convey what most of us hope will permeate the culture of our classrooms!

While many teaching practices and environmental factors contribute to a classroom culture where students feel psychologically safe and supported to ask questions, none is more important than students' deep understanding of the what and why of quality questioning practices. Three pillars support a culture that fosters student questioning. Teachers collaborate with their students to build a shared understanding of these mainstays of such a culture: (1) features and functions of quality questions, (2) the what, why, and how of think times, and (3) the value of engaging every student's voice in class interactions.

Features and Functions of Quality Questions. The first building block of a culture that invites student questions is learner understanding of the nature and purpose of questions. Far too many school children believe the sole purpose of classroom questions is the provision of answers that teachers have in mind. In these "right-answer"–oriented classrooms, usually dominated by low-level questions, most students passively observe while a small percentage of high-achieving students volunteer to respond by raising their hands.

Transforming this traditional ho-hum culture occurs only when teachers help students understand the primary purpose of questions is to advance learning. Students need to understand that teachers ask questions to find out where students are in their understanding so that they can decide what to do next to support them. In turn, students must come to believe that their questions help teachers do their jobs. Student questions not only elicit information the questioners can use to clarify and extend understandings, they also provide teachers with information that enables them to select their next best teaching move. Questions that further teacher and student learning are almost never the ones that can be googled; they are inquiries that surface the thinking behind a current understanding, whether it is correct or incorrect. When teacher questions lead to thoughtful responses and teacher words and actions convey the deeper purpose of questions, student comfort level in question-asking increases.

The What, Why, and How of Think Times. A second important feature of a culture that nurtures student questions relates to the pacing of classroom dialogue. Classroom talk in most classrooms is fast paced and dominated by the initiate-respond-evaluate (IRE) pattern, which involves the teacher asking, one student responding, and the teacher evaluating that student's answer as to its correctness. The usual time between teacher question and student answer is less than 1 second; the time between the student answer and the teacher's evaluation is infinitesimally small, oftentimes under 0 seconds because of teacher interruptions.

Most educators are familiar with this research initiated by Mary Budd Rowe in the early 1970s. She discovered the value of brief interludes of silence to student thinking and learning: an initial pause following the asking of a teacher question (Wait Time 1) and a second pause after a student answer (Wait Time 2.) Following additional research, Rowe concluded 3 to 5 seconds to be the optimal pause at both identified points of class interactions.

Over 30 years of work with K–12 teachers to change this fast-paced pattern of questioning have led me to a number of insights and strategies for changing classroom practice.

1. *Substitute* think time *for* wait time. This is particularly helpful in conversations with students because it helps them understand what to do with the pauses.

2. *You cannot "do" think times to students.* They must understand the what and the why and have opportunities for practice.

3. *Introduce appropriate hand signals or signage to support student (and your own) use.* Teachers of young students (K–3, in particular) report success in scaffolding student use by providing them with signals for the following: (1) I'm still thinking (often a fist to the chest), (2) I'm ready with a response (a thumb up on the chest); (3) I agree (back and forth motion with thumb and pinkie); (4) I have a question (2nd and 3rd finger on chest.) Different teachers adopt different signals. The important thing is that there be schoolwide consistency.

4. *Teach students the specific kind of thinking they are to do during the pauses.* Teachers have found the charts presented as Figure 1.2 and Figure 1.3 to be useful when displayed as large posters conspicuously placed on classroom walls. This signage serves as a strong reminder to both students and teacher. Additionally, teachers can point to the appropriate poster, as needed, to provide corrective feedback when students forget to pause.

5. *Engage students in periodic dialogue to help them reflect on the value of think times to their responding and on how they are progressing in their use of the two pauses for thinking.*

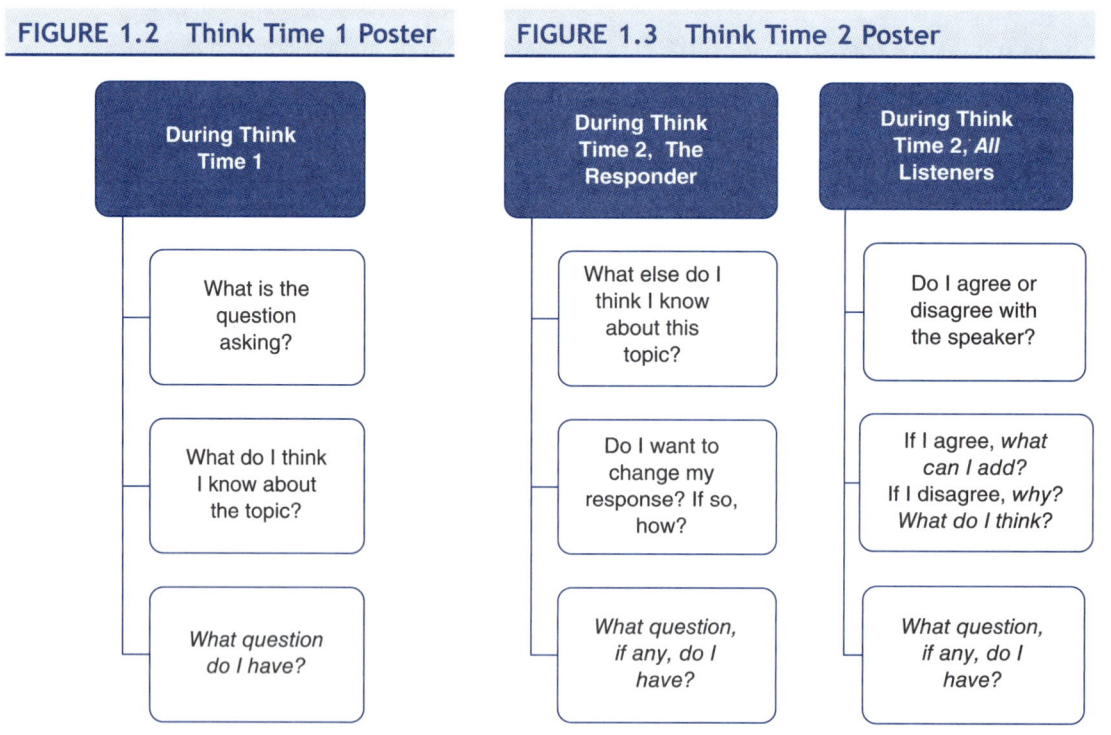

FIGURE 1.2   Think Time 1 Poster

During Think Time 1

What is the question asking?

What do I think I know about the topic?

What question do I have?

FIGURE 1.3   Think Time 2 Poster

During Think Time 2, The Responder

What else do I think I know about this topic?

Do I want to change my response? If so, how?

What question, if any, do I have?

During Think Time 2, *All* Listeners

Do I agree or disagree with the speaker?

If I agree, *what can I add?* If I disagree, *why? What do I think?*

What question, if any, do I have?

Students whose teachers provide explicit instruction about the metacognitive moves to make during the two pauses not only begin to observe the pauses (without raising hands or blurting out a response), they also respond more frequently and at greater length. The first two steps in both charts provide time for all students to process what they have heard (either the question or another student's comments) and think about what they might say in response. Students also begin asking more questions, understanding that questions are expected and valued.

Teachers who commit to prioritizing the teaching of think time and supporting their students as partners in making this change experience success, as did coteachers Jordan Whaley and Lori Woodrow featured below and in the accompanying video. The new rhythm for responding contributes to a culture that values and enables student questions (Walsh & Sattes, 2015).

> The new rhythm for responding contributes to a culture that values and enables student questions.

Student Questioners at Work

Jordan Whaley and Lori Woodrow are coteachers in a sixth-grade ELA classroom. In this inclusion class, many students are reading below grade level. Jordan and Lori made a commitment to support all of their students in becoming more effective questioners. They decided to begin by emphasizing two types of questions: self-questions and academic questions. In spite of the warm and caring relationships they had developed with their students, most students seemed afraid to pose their questions aloud in class. As these teachers reflected, they realized they were continuing to call on a small percentage of students (those who volunteered by raising their hands) to answer almost all of their questions. They also noted that these same students were the only ones who ever asked questions aloud in class and that even these students asked very few.

Jordan and Lori decided to revisit think times with their students. They used the think time posters to introduce and explicitly teach students associated metacognitive skills. Additionally, they worked

(Continued)

with students to eliminate hand-raising, to practice active listening skills, and to speak to one another (not to their teachers.) They report that the most important key to their success, however, was the time they allocated for periodic "think time" dialogues during which students reflected on their understanding of the benefits of these pauses to their thinking and learning. ■

Video 1.3: "Think Times: Key Building Blocks for Culture," features such a student dialogue.

The Value of Engaging Every Voice. The third pillar of a questioning culture relates to these questions: *Who will answer? Who will ask?* In traditional classrooms where students sit in desks in a row with all eyes on the teacher, certain students talk more than three times as much as their classmates, 25 percent of whom never participate (Sadker & Sadker, 1985). These students, dubbed *target students*, tend to sit in a particular area of the classroom designated as the *action zone*. Usually taking the shape of a "T" (with target students choosing desks across the first row and those down the center of the classroom), students in this zone are in teachers' lines of vision. Action zones are broken up with rearrangement of seating to accommodate collaborative work (e.g., students at tables or in clusters of desks). The physical arrangement of the classroom matters.

Even with strategic seating, many students, especially low achievers, opt out of classroom questioning. Teachers, under pressure to maintain pacing, often defer to the students most likely to offer a response that will move the lesson forward. A primary driver of this phenomenon is overreliance on student volunteers who typically signal their willingness to answer by hand-raising. Elimination of hand-raising is a first step toward leveling the playing field by expecting and providing opportunities for all students to participate (Walsh & Sattes, 2015; Wiliam, 2011).

What else can teachers do to level the playing field so that reticent students gain the confidence to participate—both by responding to questions and posing their own? A first step is to set expectations related to participation. Let students know that each one is responsible for using think time to either form a response or a question during the pauses following another's question or comment. Helping all students understand the primary purpose of teacher questions is important to their willingness to respond. It takes time to convince students that their teachers are not fishing for "right answers"; that more learning occurs from wrong answers than from correct ones. Many teachers find that it helps to talk with students about *forming a response*, not *answering the question*. Let them know student responses provide teachers with information about where students are in their learning, information about missing facts, or misunderstandings. Then, convince students of the value you place on their responses by asking questions to get behind their thinking—or, better yet, by helping them form questions that will elicit the help they need.

In addition to establishing a new norm related to the value of responding, teachers can select response structures and accompanying protocols that facilitate responding by all. Structures and protocols to scaffold student development of the four categories of questions are featured in the chapters that follow. Selecting an appropriate structure, one suitable for both the developmental level of your students and for the task at hand, is important to creating a culture where all feel both comfortable and accountable for asking.

HOW CAN WE DEVELOP STUDENTS' SKILL AND WILL TO ASK QUESTIONS IN CLASS? ABOUT THIS BOOK

The driving purpose for writing this book is to provide readers with strategies and structures they can use to develop students as questioners. While there are no surefire formulas or recipes, the teacher-tested methods presented are intended to provide alternatives for each reader to consider. Decisions about how to proceed with a given class of students are best made in consideration of students' age and developmental levels, the content to be learned, and teacher preferences and style.

The primary source and inspiration for the remainder of the book come from classroom teachers with whom the author has worked over the course of thirty years. These teachers have experimented with strategies and practices, offered feedback based on their experiences, shared stories of student successes, and opened their classrooms to the author. Fourteen teachers from five schools in Oxford (AL) City Schools are particularly important contributors to this book. They partnered with the author and their students to work intentionally on teaching students how to ask questions and providing time and supportive structures. These are spotlighted in stories and videos (accessible through QR Codes) spread across all chapters in the book.

Because the book is envisioned as a manual of practice for teachers, each chapter focuses on a priority for action by practitioners committed to transforming their classrooms through greater emphasis on students as questioners.

- **Chapter 2: Teachers as Activators—*Committing to Change, Creating the Culture*** acknowledges the necessity of teacher commitment to change classroom roles and responsibilities. In classrooms where students become more responsible for learning through questioning, teachers are transferring some control to the learners and teaching them how to exercise new responsibilities.

This chapter provides an eight-step process for use in teaching and reinforcing question-asking—a process that serves as an organizer for chapters that follow.

One of each of the following chapters will be dedicated to the four question types. In these chapters, readers explore specific strategies and structures for use in teaching students how to formulate and ask questions serving four distinct purposes.

- **Chapter 3: Self-Questions—*Monitoring Learning and Making Meaning*** addresses the metacognitive sphere, questions that support self-regulation and those that support individual meaning-making in different academic areas. A *Cycle of Student Self-Questioning to Learn* is a tool for fostering self-regulation. Also included is a sampling of protocols to support meaning-making in core content areas.

- **Chapter 4: Academic Questions—*Clarifying and Deepening Understanding*** features the workhorse of student classroom questions. Academic questions assist students in unpacking and better comprehending content and clearing up any confusion about procedures related to skills. This chapter addresses how to assist students in understanding differences between surface, deep, and transfer knowledge and differentiating their questions to these ends.

- **Chapter 5: Exploratory Questions—*Expressing Wonderings and Curiosities*** highlights structures and thinking routines to use in stimulating and unleashing student interests and inquisitiveness. How can teachers scaffold student generation of questions that might drive a lesson, unit of study, or an individual inquiry? While the focus is on the intentional structuring of opportunities for students to express these wonderings, considerations for inviting student curiosity in its more spontaneous, dynamic, and fluid form are also provided.

- **Chapter 6: Dialogic Questions—*Clarifying and Deepening Understanding*** spotlights questions students can use to understand different points of view or ways of approaching a problem or issue. Dialogic questions support productive conversations and enable collaborative discovery, problem-solving, and broadening of personal perspectives. Empathic listening is key to the forming of questions that seek to make assumptions transparent and get behind the why of another's claim.

- **Chapter 7: The End in Mind: *Increased Agency Within and Beyond the Classroom*** illustrates the interconnectedness of the four question types, emphasizing that these do not operate in isolation, rather in a complementary fashion. This short chapter also reinforces the vision for classrooms where students develop the skill, will, and thrill to use questions to advance their own and their classmates' learning, preparing for success in their unpredictable futures.

- **A special feature of Chapters 2–6** is a spotlight on opportunities for student questions in the online environment. These focus on the purpose for eliciting the designated question type during virtual learning and identify a sampling of strategies, structures, and apps to support the purpose.

In Closing: *Changing the Equation*

Student questions have the potential to change the teaching-learning equation, to place emphasis on learning, not only on teaching. When this occurs, many benefits accrue to students and teachers. This transformation does not occur spontaneously. Teachers must be committed to changing the traditional classroom dynamic, first by helping students develop the requisite knowledge and skills of effective questioners. In the process, students and teachers will adopt new mindframes and cocreate classroom cultures where student questioning can thrive.

Curtain Call: Revisiting Key Ideas Related to Student Questions

KEY IDEAS	QUESTIONS FOR PERSONAL REFLECTION
1. Question-asking contributes to student success in school and beyond.	• Do you agree or disagree with this premise? Which identified benefits to students do you most value? • What other benefits to students (not identified in this chapter) can you suggest?
2. Student question-asking supports teachers' ability to support the learning of each student.	• Which of the benefits to teachers identified in this chapter do you most value? • Can you remember a time as a teacher when a student question helped you better understand how you might support her learning?
3. Most students believe their role is to answer, not ask, questions in class.	• In your experience, have you found this statement to be mostly true? • Why do you think students hold this attitude?
4. Because many students possess neither the skills nor the will to ask questions, teachers must cultivate both of these if they value student questions.	• Do you agree that most students lack the skill and the will to ask questions in class? What makes you think this? • How might you convince a colleague of the need to spend time developing student question-asking skills?
5. Four categories of questions support student learning in class: self-questions, academic questions, exploratory questions, and dialogic questions.	• Reflect on your experience with student learning. Do you agree that these four types of questions support learners? • Which of these question types do you believe are most and least used by students you have known? How do you explain this?
6. When students believe that teachers and classmates value their questions, they develop the will to ask.	• What evidence, if any, can you offer to support this claim? • What ideas do you have for communicating to students the value of their questions?
7. Student understanding and acceptance of three quality questioning practices contribute to a culture where student questions are valued.	• How might movement away from a "right-answer" classroom encourage student questions? • Reflect on possible connections between the strategic use of think times and the quantity and quality of student questions in a class. • Which learners might benefit most from transforming a classroom culture to one supportive of student questions? What makes you think this?

Teachers as Activators

*Committing to Change,
Creating the Culture*

I cultivate student questions
that spark thinking
and learning.

TEACHER MINDFRAME

Changing student perceptions and behaviors in classrooms begins with changing teacher beliefs and assumptions. This is a simple but challenging process. Innate within all learners is a natural curiosity, the propensity to ask questions that fuel the process of making meaning of one's environment, experiences, and new information. Traditional classroom rules and roles suppress this universal motivator of learning, depriving students of the confidence required to ask rather than answer, to view not knowing as an opportunity to learn rather than a sign of failure. Consider the potential of this teacher mindframe for transforming classroom rules and roles. *I cultivate student questions that spark thinking and learning.*

> "In order not to squash what comes naturally to students, we must allow for what . . . John Dewey (2013) called venturing into the unknown. This represents a shift in the way we see the traditional role of a teacher, from one who asks and answers questions to one who elicits them." (Ostroff, 2016, p. 7)

At the heart of this way of thinking is the belief that student questions are the gateway to enhanced thinking and learning. This mindframe also assumes that teachers are able to nurture students as questioners, to create an environment or culture in which student curiosity thrives. Further, this mindframe requires strategies and tools for use in enhancing students' capacity to question.

HOW CAN TEACHERS MOTIVATE STUDENTS? CREATING THE CLASSROOM CULTURE

A CLASSROOM PORTRAIT

Tracy Ray, third-grade science teacher, believes that student questions can be powerful drivers of their learning. To create an environment in which her students also will come to believe in the value of their questions, she adopted the theme,

"I mustache a question" and fashioned and cut out mustaches to hang from the classroom ceiling. As she had predicted, her students' curiosity was piqued; they asked, "Why did you hang mustaches from the ceiling?" Mrs. Ray challenged them to keep asking questions and to discover the answers to this mystery. Their conversations that week were priceless.

She heard comments like: "Maybe she just wanted to redecorate." "Are we getting a student teacher who has a mustache?" "Is it Cinco de Mayo?" "I went to a mustache-themed party last year. . . ." "Maybe the mustaches are for a class party."

After a week of student wondering, she came to school one day sporting her own mustache and unveiled a new class motto: "I mustache [must ask] a question." She then engaged the students in dialogue about the importance and value of questions to their learning.

Mrs. Ray had already been partnering with her students to create norms and practices supporting quality questioning. Her students understood that the primary purpose of questions is to assess and advance learning, not to surface "right answers." They had become comfortable with silence and knew how to use think times to ponder questions and surface prior understandings. They had learned to raise their hands only when they had questions to ask, not answers to offer. They were developing a classroom community in which they valued listening to and learning from one another, where they respected different ways of thinking, and where they were comfortable responding even when they weren't sure of the correctness of their thinking. However, they had not yet begun thinking of themselves as questioners; they continued to view themselves as responders to their teachers' questions. Mrs. Ray hoped to change this mindset over time.

> "We take it as axiomatic that the attitudes of teachers are the most important characteristic of the inquiry environment. *There can be no significant innovation in education that does not have at its center the attitudes of teachers, and it is an illusion to think otherwise.* The beliefs, feelings, and assumptions of teachers are the air of a learning environment; they determine the quality of life within it." (Postman & Weingartner, 1969, p. 33)

LEADING THE WAY

Teachers cannot create classroom cultures on their own; culture creation is a community process. Teachers are, however, the principals in this process; they lead the way. How can teachers create classroom cultures that support student wondering, that invite students to voice their questions? While there's no magic wand or sure-fire formula, a number of general principles can help chart a course.

- *Imagine It.* Classroom culture begins and depends upon a teacher's personal vision of a way of being together. *How do I want my students to feel when they walk into my classroom? In what ways do I hope they will interact with me? How do I imagine them relating to one another?*

- *Own It.* Are you imagining a classroom where students are comfortable, one where they feel physically and psychologically safe? Do you value two-way communications buttressed by active and empathic listening, deepened by questioning for understanding, and expanded by collaborative thinking? Do you visualize relationships woven together by honesty, respect, trust, and empathy? Do you hope that students will adopt a stance of curiosity and inquisitiveness, a posture of reflecting and wondering, a mindset of questioning themselves, ideas and phenomena, and one another? If so, ask yourself what you are doing to model, nurture, support, and sustain these dispositions and behaviors—and what might you be doing to discourage them. Ask yourself what else you might do to model, nurture, support, and sustain this vision.

- *Structure It.* Investigate structures, including procedures and protocols that you might intentionally use to scaffold student behaviors and that you might adopt to create fields of practice that enable students to act their way into new ways of thinking and behaving with automaticity.

- *Spotlight It.* Be transparent with your students about what you're hoping to cocreate with them. Ask them what supports their feelings of comfort, confidence, and curiosity—and what gets in the way of these feelings. Listen to their perspectives. Codevelop a list of expectations they're willing to accept for themselves and support in others. Agree upon goals or targets.

- *Celebrate It.* Reinforce students when they meet expectations. Provide time for individual and collective reflection on how things are going, on progress toward meeting expectations and goals. Invite students to celebrate with you and one another collective successes.

How Should Teachers Proceed?
Setting Explicit Expectations

COMMITTING TO INTENTIONAL INSTRUCTION

Many have written about children's natural propensity to ask questions, about their instinctive curiosity. I do not challenge this premise. I am a mother and grandmother who observed my children learn through questioning. The first complete sentences formed by Catherine, my eldest, were questions: *Who's that? What's that?* She was constantly asking even before her first birthday. Children do naturally ask questions as they seek to make meaning of their environment. Perhaps because of this, some argue that all students could be effective questioners in school if teachers would but allow this. This claim is not well-substantiated.

Innate curiosity does not always transfer into children knowing how to ask the kinds of questions that advance academic learning or enable understanding of different perspectives. Kindergarten teachers report that many of their young students don't know the difference between a question and a statement and certainly don't understand how questions can support their learning. Likewise, many secondary teachers claim not to see evidence of students asking productive classroom questions.

> Innate curiosity does not always transfer into children knowing how to ask the kinds of questions that advance academic learning or enable understanding of different perspectives.

Researchers have found that low-achieving students are less likely to ask questions than their high-achieving classmates as they progress through school. One sad and startling research finding is that these students asked as many questions as their classmates when in kindergarten, but as upper elementary and secondary pupils they asked significantly fewer (Good & Brophy, 1991). O'Keefe (1995) argues that this contributes to the passivity that results in low levels of engagement and subsequent low achievement.

These observations and findings lead to the underlying premise of this book: Most students can benefit from explicit and intentional instruction in question-asking *when it is integrated into ongoing teaching and learning*. This caveat is important: Skill development in question-asking needs to be embedded in

> Most students can benefit from explicit and intentional instruction in question-asking *when it is integrated into ongoing teaching and learning*.

the context of a daily lesson so that students are clear about the purpose for which they are being encouraged to form and pose their questions.

Student Questioners at Work

Fourth-grade ELA teacher Brittany Pinkard committed to greater intentionality in developing the questioning skills of her young students. After identifying the need to scaffold their understanding of the features of a quality question, she provided them with a student-friendly set of criteria to support their question formation. She integrates opportunities for them to apply these new understandings into their daily lessons.

Brittany is mindful of the importance of creating a classroom environment in which students feel comfortable asking questions. She also values the student mainframes as a tool to remind them of why forming questions is important to their learning.

In Video 2.2, "What Makes a Question a Quality One?" students are rotating through stations where they analyze questions to

(Continued)

(Continued)

determine if they meet the criteria for a quality question. The students collaboratively analyze and discuss teacher-developed questions related to an informational text they have read. They first decide if each question meets the criteria for a quality question; then they respond to the question. At one station, each group has an opportunity to create their own questions about the text and receive feedback from their teacher when she meet with her. ■

AN INFORMAL ASSESSMENT TO FOSTER AWARENESS

Figure 2.1a presents an Informal Inventory of Student Question-Asking for use in grades 4 through 12; Figure 2.1b offers a modified version for use in K–3. Such an assessment of student perceptions of their question-asking behaviors can serve multiple purposes. First and perhaps most important, this short inventory focuses student attention on the range of questions that can support them as learners. Many students have no reason to believe that teachers are interested in their questions. This inventory conveys that interest and encourages students to reflect on whether and when they pose questions in class. Second, the results of the inventory provide the teacher with a sense of what their students believe about their role as questioners. Finally, teachers can use specific items as discussion starters when setting expectations for student questioning in their classroom.

You are invited to adapt the appropriate inventory for use with your class. Consider administering the inventory early in the school term as you introduce students to expectations related to their questioning and at appropriate intervals to measure changes in their perceptions.

How Can Teachers Transform Learning? A Process to Build Capacity

Some students arrive at school armed with both the skills and the dispositions equipping them to become effective questioners. Questioning appears to be in their DNA. On the other hand, many of their peers don't know how to begin or how to express their confusion or curiosity.

One factor constraining a student's ability to ask questions is requisite background knowledge. Dillon (1988) observed that in order to ask a question, one needs to know two-thirds of the answer. While he does not offer data to support this

FIGURE 2.1A   Informal Inventory of Student Question-Asking

Grades 6–12

Directions: Carefully read each of the questions below. Using the following scale for your answers, circle your response. Please answer as honestly as possible.

1 = I almost never do this.

2 = I do this occasionally.

3 = I do this fairly often.

4 = I almost always do this.

When thinking of your response, consider all of your classroom experiences over the past several years—in all subject areas with all teachers. This is not about your experience in this class only.

1. I ask questions publicly *during whole-class instruction* when I am confused about a concept or don't know where to begin solving a problem.	1	2	3	4
2. I ask questions of my teachers *privately* when I am confused about a concept or procedure.	1	2	3	4
3. I ask questions in class when I don't understand a teacher's directions.	1	2	3	4
4. When I am reading a text or listening to a teacher explain something in class, I ask questions to myself to better understand.	1	2	3	4
5. I ask and answer questions that help me self-assess, monitor my progress, and decide on what to do next in learning.	1	2	3	4
6. During class discussions, I ask my classmates questions when I disagree with them or don't understand why they think the way they do.	1	2	3	4
7. I ask questions when I am curious about something related to a subject I'm studying, when I just wonder about something.	1	2	3	4
8. After classes are over, I sometimes think of questions related to topics we are studying.	1	2	3	4
9. I ask questions of my parents and other family members when I am curious or want to know how to do something.	1	2	3	4
10. I ask questions of my friends (outside of school) when I am curious about why they think or behave as they do or when I want to know how to do something.	1	2	3	4

FIGURE 2.1B Student Survey

Informal Inventory of Student Question-Asking, Grades K–3

Directions: Teacher reads aloud each item, pausing to allow students adequate time to mark their response forms.

If you agree with a statement, put an "x" in the box beneath

If you disagree with a statement, put an "x" in the box beneath

If you're not sure about a statement, put an "x" in the box beneath

	I AGREE	I DISAGREE	I'M NOT SURE
1. I ask my teacher questions when I'm confused about what I'm learning.			
2. I ask my teacher questions when I don't understand the directions.			
3. I ask questions to myself when I am reading or trying to work a math problem.			
4. I ask my classmates questions when I don't understand something.			
5. I ask myself questions when I am self-assessing my progress.			
6. I ask my classmates questions when I disagree with them.			
7. I ask questions at home when I am curious or wonder about something.			
8. I ask my friends questions when we are not in school if I need to find out something or want to know what they think.			

assertion, it does ring true. Certainly, most of us are not tempted to ask questions about rocket science—or what goes on inside of our computers for that matter! We simply don't know enough to formulate a question on these topics. We'll leave Dillon's claim for

the moment (and return to it in Chapter 4) and turn to what teachers can do to develop the will and the skill of all students to ask questions in service of their learning.

Developing student capacity to ask questions requires both commitment and a plan. Figure 2.2 illustrates an eight-step process that involves teachers in preparing students (focusing on mindframes, teaching strategies and stems, and modeling through think-alouds); designing lessons (adopting routines and protocols and integrating into daily lessons); and engaging students in forming and asking (making time and space, affording practice with feedback, and inviting reflection.) These eight activities are appropriate for use in developing all four of the question types included in the Taxonomy. They will provide a common organization to the four chapters that follow.

FIGURE 2.2 A Process to Build Capacity

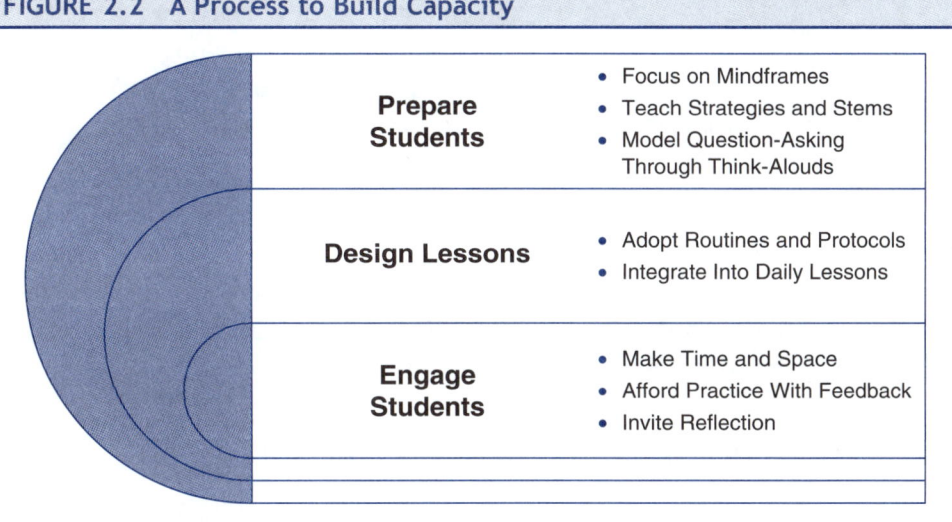

FOCUS ON MINDFRAMES

For each question type, there is a companion mindframe to facilitate student understanding of the primary reason for asking the related category of question. Teachers who have worked with these mindframes create anchor charts or posters for public display of each mindframe. Such visuals serve to remind students of the value of asking questions while engaging in a given learning task.

When first introducing a mindframe, invite students to unpack the statement and explore the meaning of each key word. Engage students in reflection and dialogue to make personal meaning of the purpose behind this question type.

Each time you begin a lesson segment, point to the related question type on the anchor chart as a reminder to students of the kinds of questions they may wish to generate. For example, at the beginning of a daily lesson, point to self-questions as a reminder to students to ask themselves such questions as, *What am I learning today? What do I already know related to the learning goals?* and so forth.

TEACH STRATEGIES AND STEMS

Each question type has a particular structure and grammar, specific characteristics or traits. These will be presented along with prompts and stems that students can adapt for use. Additionally, you will find alternative strategies students can use in the creation and assessment of their own and their peers' questions.

The ideal is to establish a school-wide goal of developing student capacity as questioners. A productive activity for a faculty is the collaborative development of a continuum for the introduction and teaching of skills associated with each question type. Teachers can then agree upon a progression of exemplars and stems to support student development at every grade level.

MODEL QUESTION-ASKING THROUGH THINK-ALOUDS

Teachers are accustomed to asking questions during class. The vast majority of these questions focus on surface knowledge, at the DOK 1 or Revised Bloom Remember levels. These are not the types of questions for which students need more models. Rather, they need to hear teachers pose questions that encourage reflection, clarification of thinking, understanding of a speaker's thinking, or expression of curiosity. Modeling and demonstration, when accompanied by an explanation of the thinking behind the question, is the most powerful form of instruction.

ADOPT ROUTINES AND PROTOCOLS

New behaviors can become routinized via scaffolding. Scaffolds are structures that support student development of new skills and knowledge. In the case of question-asking, teachers can draw from a body of thinking routines (e.g., Richhart, Church, & Morrison, 2011) and available protocols. Best practice is for teachers to select a limited number of such structures that are appropriate to their grade level and content area. Teach students the procedures associated with each selected routine or protocol and plan to use on a regular basis. When students become familiar with frequently used structures, a minimum amount of time is dedicated to procedural and logistical issues.

INCORPORATE INTO DAILY LESSONS

What gets planned in advance usually gets done during a lesson. The reverse is also true. Teacher commitment to student questions is evidenced by their inclusion in daily lesson plans. Lesson planning begins with a focus on standards and learning goals. Beginning with Grade 2, most state language arts standards include a focus on asking and answering questions of texts and of speakers during a class discussion (http://www.corestandards.org/ELA-Literacy/SL/2/.) Teachers who are intentionally developing students as questioners integrate this skill into their daily learning targets or intentions.

Student Questioners at Work

Creating learning targets/ intentions that drive a lesson is appropriate across all grade levels. These set the stage for a lesson by focusing student attention on the expectation that one of their primary roles in an upcoming lesson is to form their own questions.

Examples of such learning targets across multiple grade levels and disciplines appear in the Video 2.3, "How Can Questioning Skills Be Woven Into Daily Learning Targets?" ∎

The mindset introduced at the beginning of this chapter—*I cultivate student questions that spark thinking and learning*—can be an important consideration during lesson planning.

When imagining a daily lesson, we can ask such questions as, *At what turns in this lesson would the opportunity to frame and ask questions of their own advance student learning? When can I invite students to form questions rather than answering my questions?* Certain types of student questions advance particular lesson goals.

MAKE TIME AND SPACE

This is a two-pronged issue. On the one hand, there are issues related to structured opportunities for students to work on question preparation. One important skill in lesson design is the estimation and allocation of adequate time for students to think and work through such a task. During the apprentice stages of question formulation, students obviously need more time to conceptualize and form questions. As they become more facile in the process, they will create questions with greater automaticity. Regardless of student skill level, teachers are required to make decisions as to the proper placement within a lesson of routines and protocols supporting question formulation.

> During the apprentice stages of question formulation, students obviously need more time to conceptualize and form questions. As they become more facile in the process, they will create questions with greater automaticity.

The second prong of the time and space issue depends upon the rhythm of a classroom. If the teacher dominates talk time and if the pacing of class interactions is rapid fire in nature, there is little opportunity for students to engage in the reflection requisite to the forming of a productive question or to gain the floor to pose their questions. Enter Think Times 1 and 2. Following a question posed by a teacher or student, a pause of only 3 to 5 seconds can afford time for all students to form a question to clarify what is being asked (Think Time 1.) And after a comment or response from another, intentional silence offers time for listeners to process the statement, form and ask questions that may advance understanding, or question assumptions and evidence. Researchers have consistently found that these two pauses result in an increased number of student questions (Rowe, 1986; Tobin, 1987). While think times afford a break in action, a safe and inquiry-oriented classroom environment provides the space.

AFFORD PRACTICE WITH FEEDBACK

When learning new routines and skills, students benefit from structured practice with feedback. Early in the learning, teachers provide almost all of the feedback related to the quality of student questions. Feedback is more productive when related to a predetermined list of success criteria associated with question types. Suggested success criteria will be offered in the chapters to come. Teachers can customize these to their students and content area and introduce these to students as part of the learning process. Repeated use will reinforce for students the qualities of effective questions. As students develop knowledge of the criteria of effective questions, teachers can structure opportunities for students to provide feedback to one another.

Student Questioners at Work

Student questions drive learning for third graders in Tracy Ray's science class.

Almost every day these learners have opportunities to record their own wonderings in their science journals. They also collaboratively generate questions as they engage in whole-class discussions. At a strategic point in a unit, they have the opportunity to review all of their questions and use criteria to select one for individual or collaborative investigation. They are also learning how to select "Reliable Sources" to use in their investigations. Students have time to pursue their inquiries during center time, working independently but with guidance from their teacher. Using this process, Mrs. Ray guides students in leading their own learning.

As they form questions to deepen their understanding of the academic content under study, their teacher offers structures, time, and coaching to assist. In this videotaped lesson, students are using an adaptation of *The Questioning Continuum* (Quigley) to assess their questions by interest and complexity. They engage in collaborative dialogue to provide feedback to one another. ∎

Video 2.4: "Peer Feedback for Student Questions"

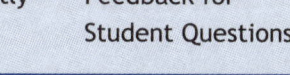

INVITE REFLECTION

To become more effective questioners, students must develop the habit of reflection to gauge their progress. Teachers facilitate reflection by providing students with time and structures to support the process. Some teachers ask their students to keep a "Question Journal" for tracking questions that occur to them spontaneously and those that result from teacher-provided opportunities to form and record questions. Periodically, they ask their students to look back through these to classify them as to type (i.e., self-, academic, dialogic, exploratory) as well as to quality (using a list of success criteria). Additionally, students can occasionally be prompted to reflect on the extent to which they are using various mindframes and identify evidence they have of such use.

Not only is it important to encourage student reflection on individual progress, collaborative reflection on the evolution of question-asking across a community of learners can also be fruitful. Teachers can participate in and scaffold such class discussions, reinforcing growth and assisting the class in setting new goals.

In Closing: *Changing the Equation*

Many accept the age-old adage that the teacher's job is to ask questions and the students' job is to answer. This assumes answering questions leads to learning.

Some believe that students who wish to ask questions can do so in response to the familiar classroom refrain: *Do you have any questions?* This assumes that students *know enough* to ask, that they *know how* to ask, and that they have the courage to ask.

What if these assumptions are incorrect? Imagine that students learn more from asking than from answering. Imagine that students can be taught how to form questions to support their learning. Imagine they can cocreate a classroom community where they are comfortable and confident posing questions. If you can embrace these possibilities, you are poised to embark on the learning journey that unfolds in the chapters to come.

Spotlight: Online Opportunities for Student Questions

The online environment provides a space in which students can record and share their questions as well as one where teachers can nurture and support students as they develop questioning skills. Many teachers use online platforms and apps to extend opportunities for student participation during traditional, face-to-face learning. Recognizing and using this environment assumes even greater importance when learners are engaged through distance and hybrid learning.

A special feature of each of the next four chapters will be a spotlight on how teachers can structure opportunities for student questions during online learning. Most of the principles and practices apply whether students are physically present in a classroom or in a remote location. Particular attention, however, will be given to ways in which teachers can support students when they are learning remotely. Each spotlight will address the following considerations.

Begin with the end in mind. What functions and potential learning outcomes will the forming and posing of this type of question support? While tech tools can introduce novelty to the completion of a task and thereby engage students for the moment, they should not be used as ends to themselves but as means to advancement of an identified learning goal (i.e., target or intention). Consider the desired outcomes for your students, given their age and the content area you teach, before considering tools.

Highlight the appropriate mindframe, skills, and tools for students in the lesson where particular question types will be emphasized. Mindframes assist students in understanding why their questions are important to their learning. Stems and strategies enable them to enhance their skills in forming questions. When working online, they are no less in need of anchor charts to gently remind them of expectations and routines to support their question-asking than when they are together in a physical classroom. Determining where to house tools, including stems/prompts and criteria for effective questions, is important.

Strategically position formal requests for student questions in the unit or lesson. To optimize the benefits of student questions, attempt to seamlessly insert formal requests for these into the flow of a unit and its component lessons.

Adapt protocols and response routines for online use. Structures and formats to guide thinking and responding support cognitive functioning in all settings but are especially critical when students are working independently. When students move from face-to-face to virtual learning, it is smart to adapt protocols and routines with which they are already familiar and to carefully select a limited number of these structures so as to minimize management problems.

Carefully select a limited number of tech tools (i.e., platforms and apps) for use by a class of students. Limiting the number

(Continued)

(Continued)

and relying on the familiar applies here as well. While it may be tempting to introduce a line-up of new apps, students (and their parents) are better able to focus on the substance of learning when not overwhelmed by new technical or procedural issues. No attempt has been made to provide an exhaustive list of tech tools in the *Spotlights* in upcoming chapters. Rather, I've chosen to highlight how representative tools might be employed in service of supporting different types of student questions in the virtual environment. You can easily transfer these ideas to your favorite tools.∎

Curtain Call: Revisiting Key Ideas Related to Teachers as Activators

KEY IDEAS	QUESTIONS FOR PERSONAL REFLECTION
1. Traditional classroom rules, roles, and structures do not nurture, support, and invite student questions.	• Do you agree or disagree with this premise? What evidence supports your response? • What do you believe to be the most important changes that teachers can make to increase the number of productive questions asked by students?
2. Teacher Mindframe: *I cultivate student questions that spark thinking and learning.*	• What does this mindframe mean to you? How do you interpret it? • Surface your beliefs about the value of student questions and their role in learning. To what extent are they aligned with this mindframe?
3. Most students can benefit from an intentional, explicit focus on the development of their questioning skills.	• In your experience, have you found this statement to be mostly true? • Why do you believe many students lack the skills associated with the forming of effective questions?
4. A supportive classroom culture is a necessary condition for student question-asking, and teachers need to lead the way in cocreating such a culture with their students.	• Why might it be important for teachers to "cocreate" supportive cultures with their students? • What is your reaction to the five principles for use by teachers in cocreating a culture that supports students as questioners? • Which of the five do you believe would present the greatest challenge to most teachers?
5. An informal inventory of student perceptions related to the asking of questions can be a useful first step in the process of developing student capacity.	• Review the sample inventory provided as Figure 2.1. In what ways do you think this might serve as a helpful tool in kicking off an effort to enhance student question-asking in a classroom? • How, if at all, might you modify this inventory for use with your students?
6. Eight discrete activities are associated with a process that teachers can use to develop their students' capacity as questioners.	• Which activity (or activities) do you believe might present the greatest challenge to you and your colleagues? • What might be the value of using this process to develop a map or plan for activating students as questioners in your school or classroom?
7. If students are to use questions more effectively to support their learning, teachers need to commit for the long haul.	• What might increase the probability of long-term commitment to the goal of enhancing students' questioning-asking capacity? • What might be the pay-off of such long-term commitment?

CHAPTER 3

Self-Questions

*Monitoring Learning and
Making Meaning*

> I ask questions to
> myself to reflect on
> and monitor my thinking
> and learning.

> I ask questions to figure
> out the meaning of what
> I am reading or hearing
> and to think through
> problems and tasks.

STUDENT MINDFRAMES

Student Questioners at Work

Self-questions serve a range of purposes. Important among these is student use to monitor their own thinking before speaking as they engage in collaborative problem-solving. This is particularly important in design thinking, whatever the product of the design may be. In this short video clip, student members of a high school green car design team reflect on the value of self-questions to the process of continually testing and improving the efficiency, safety, and overall effectiveness of their cars. The skillful use of questions enables this team to engage in productive collaborative dialogue by respectfully listening to, reflecting on, and considering ideas different from their own. ■

Video 3.1: "The Value of Questions in Design Thinking"

All questions sprout from seeds of confusion or curiosity that germinate within the mind. Some blossom and emerge as spoken words intended to elicit responses from others. Other questions are generated for self, to support the creator's thinking, learning, and functioning. These latter type questions, self-questions, are the drivers of self-regulation and meaning-making. They are metacognitive in nature.

> "The most effective student we know of is a self-questioning one. A learner who can pose questions to herself and act upon the answers is one who is virtually unstoppable. The ability to do so is one that develops through lots of opportunities to engage in self-reflection and self-questioning, which has an effect size of $d = 0.64$ (Hattie, as cited in Frey, Hattie, & Fisher, 2018, p. 98).

When individuals become deliberate and intentional in questioning themselves, they develop an important metacognitive skill. When students ask these kinds of questions routinely, they are able to monitor their progress toward learning goals and check their understanding of both the written and spoken word as well as of other audio and visual stimuli. When adults master these skills, they better manage almost all aspects of their lives.

How People Learn (Bransford, Brown, & Cocking, 2000) established the importance of the metacognitive approach in "help[ing] students learn to take control of their own learning by defining learning goals and monitoring their progress toward achieving them" (p. 18). The authors of this report argue for the integration of the metacognitive into the curriculum as a way of increasing achievement and developing independent learners. They associate student questioning with the development of student metacognitive skills.

John Hattie's extensive synthesis (2009) affirms the impact of metacognitive strategies on student achievement ($d = 0.69$). Hattie's analysis also validated the value of self-questioning, revealing an effect size of $d = 0.64$. Given the $d = 0.40$ hinge point (meaning one year's growth for one year of schooling), the potential impact of self-questioning cannot be overstated. While the teaching of self-questions has a positive impact on the learning of all students, numerous studies have found that the impact is even greater for low-achievers (e.g., Bransford, Brown, & Cocking, 2000; Ostroff, 2016).

For purposes of planning and integration of metacognitive questions into instruction, this question type is broken into two categories: self-regulation questions and questions that promote meaning-making. Self-regulation questions are used to self-assess, monitor, and regulate thinking and learning. Meaning-making self-questions support comprehension of the written or spoken word or of other visual or auditory input, helping students better comprehend the content they are studying. Haller, Child, and Walberg (1988) found the effect size of metacognitive strategies on reading comprehension to be $d = 0.71$. These researchers reported student use of self-questioning to be one of the most effective metacognitive strategies investigated.

MONITORING LEARNING—DEVELOPING STUDENT CAPACITY TO ASK QUESTIONS TO SELF-REGULATE

Teacher Reflection

"I recently had a moment of epiphany with my biology class. We've adopted proficiency scales and learning target trackers as tools for student progress-monitoring. The challenge for students is to use these to self-assess, to ask questions about their own learning. I know this is a hard task, but my expectation was that they would do better than they were.

"Initially, students had a difficult time shifting from grade-focused to standards-based thinking about progress. They tended to ask questions such as *Why didn't I do well? Why did this happen to me? Why won't he give me a better grade?* When I stopped to provide some explicit instruction on stems and prompts that focused them on the what of their learning, they became much more successful. Questions that have promoted more productive reflections include: *What do I know? What did I not do well on? What is confusing me? What can I do differently next time?* Asking these self-questions, students are making better use of the proficiency scale as a tool for learning.

"I've learned that most students don't quite know how to ask themselves questions about their learning. Even high school freshmen need to be taught."—Britton Young, ninth-grade biology teacher ■

Self-regulation is the element of metacognition that relates to "the capacity to reflect on and monitor one's own cognitive processes" (The National Academies of Sciences-Engineering-Medicine, 2018, p. 73). Learners can best till this area of the metacognitive by routinely asking themselves questions to reflect on both *the what* and *the how* of their learning. Such questions do not come automatically to most students. Teachers can scaffold their development using the process described in the previous chapter (Figure 2.2, A Process to Build Capacity) to do so.

> **Begin With the Mindframe:** *I ask questions to myself to reflect on and monitor my thinking and learning.*

Ask students what this statement means to them. *What do "reflection" and "monitoring of thinking and learning" communicate to them?* Give them a moment to think and jot down their ideas; then ask them to share their thoughts with a partner. Call on students to share their partners' thinking. Chart their responses. Look for patterns. What emerges? Now ask the partners to generate strategies they might use to monitor their learning. Again, facilitate sharing out. Lead the class in discussing why such monitoring might be important to them. Post this mindframe or create an anchor chart displaying it. Tell students they will be exploring strategies and developing skills they can use to engage in this process.

TEACH A STRATEGY FOR SELF-REGULATION

For many students, self-regulation is a foreign territory. They do not know how to navigate this learning terrain because they've never been taught—either explicitly or through modeling. Current literature is replete with approaches to develop the metagcognitive. The Cycle of Student Self-Questioning to Learn, Figure 2.1, represents a synthesis of thinking across the field. The cycle illustrates strategic points in the learning process for student self-questioning and includes focus questions for use at these six key points. These questions, which provide definition for each stage, can serve as pathways for student self-regulation at progressive junctures in the learning process. If you have embraced a cycle for student metacognition, reflect on how you might scaffold student self-questions with the cycle. If you are not currently using a systemic approach to support this important area of learning, consider the value of offering students the cycle as a tool for self-regulation.

> For many students, self-regulation is a foreign territory.

Through the mindframe discussion, you can engage students in thinking about the importance of self-questioning to the monitoring of their learning. Segue from this broader focus into a presentation of the six-staged cycle (displayed in Figure 3.1) by guiding student thinking about each of the six questions, in turn. Assist students in translating these standard questions into more age-appropriate language, if need be, and in generating related, supportive questions.

FIGURE 3.1   Cycle of Student Self-Questioning to Learn*

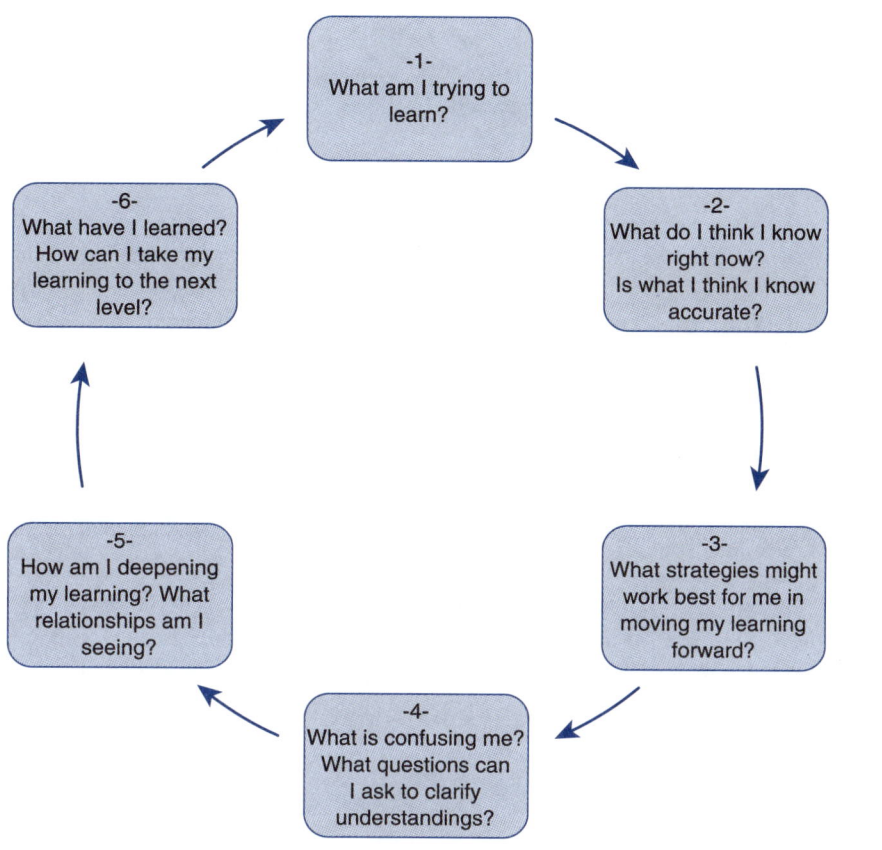

*Adapted from Walsh, J. A., & Sattes, B. D., (2011). *Thinking through quality questioning* (p. 8). Thousand Oaks, CA: Corwin.

You may wish to coconstruct this cycle with your students, introducing one or two chunks at a time. Designate a wall space for "building" this cycle, placing arrows strategically and leaving spaces to place the six blocks as you introduce each.

Begin with a focus on the first two stages, sharing visuals representing each. Post the first key question, "What am I trying to learn?"

- *What am I trying to learn?* This question is the essential springboard for student entry into each new lesson. If learners are to manage and self-regulate their progress, they must understand the intended learning goals from the outset. This is key to student ownership of their learning and of their ability to seek and use feedback from others. Help students connect this question to their daily learning targets.

  Point to a learning target for the current lesson and request that students silently translate that target into their own words. Then ask that they turn to assigned thinking partners to exchange understandings.

As you debrief with the whole class, ask them how they defined key words in the target. Did their understanding match that of their partners? Suggest that they focus on daily learning targets as they enter the classroom each day, knowing that you'll be asking them to express in their own words what they will be learning during the lesson or class period.

Now, turn student attention to the second key question.

- *What do I think I know right now? Is what I think I know accurate?* When students enter the learning process by asking these questions, they activate prior knowledge, calling to mind experiences and understandings they connect to the new learning target. As they reflect on the questions, they need to be mindful of the importance of inquiring into whether their prior knowledge and preconceptions are correct. If accurate, the learner can build on this prior knowledge, deepening and extending understandings. If misconceptions exist, this is the point in the learning cycle to surface these and seek clarification.

Teacher questions and structures serve to scaffold student ability to engage independently in the asking and answering of these pre-assessment questions. Early on in this process, however, it is equally important to help students understand why the activation and verification of prior knowledge is important. Again, turn to a daily learning target and invite them to reflect and jot down what they think they already know that might relate to this target. You may wish to use one of the routines or protocols listed below to structure this thinking. Scan student responses to identify both correct and incorrect ideas that may have surfaced. Use selected responses as examples to help students understand how to work through this phase.

The next set of questions are the workhorses of student metacognition. Strategy selection, use, and assessment are fundamental to success in meeting learning targets.

- *What strategies might work best for me at this point in the learning? What assistance, if any, do I need to get started or make adjustments?* In the posing of the previous questions, the learner focuses on *the what* of the learning. With these questions, *the how* of learning comes to the fore. Effective learners possess a repertoire of learning strategies for each academic discipline. During this step, they access possible strategies and determine which to try first. If they are stuck, unsure of how to proceed, they know to ask for assistance in choosing a strategy—as opposed to asking for "the answer" to the problem or question.

When introducing these questions, it is important to assist students in surfacing the strategies they have in their arsenal for the content area or discipline under study. Talk to them about the necessity of continually asking, "How is this working?" "Is there another way to attack this task or problem?" Elementary teachers might initially provide their students with lists of strategies available to them for different purposes. Secondary teachers, on the other hand, can facilitate student generation of strategies they are bringing with them from past years of schooling while providing them with new approaches.

Students need to understand the need to keep these questions in the forefront of their thinking throughout a learning sequence. Strategy selection can sometimes be a trial-and-error process. In this way, students learn to constantly adjust their learning based upon the feedback generated by these questions.

Even as students monitor *the how* of their learning by focusing on strategies, they continue thinking about the what or the content to be mastered by asking:

- *What is confusing to me? What questions do I need to ask?* The metacognitive learner uses both the learning target and success criteria to monitor progress and identify points of confusion. As they identify areas of uncertainty or misunderstanding, they begin to form academic questions to ask aloud to their teacher or peers.

The next questions require greater sophistication on the part of students and are beyond the capacity of many younger learners. As students develop cognitively, it is important to offer them explicit questions for assessing their readiness to go beyond the surface to deep knowledge. Introducing the following questions is a good beginning point for increasing capacity in this area.

> As students develop cognitively, it is important to offer them explicit questions for assessing their readiness to go beyond surface to deep knowledge.

- *How am I deepening my learning? What relationships am I seeing?* As students progress in the learning of factual and procedural knowledge, they benefit from structures and prompts that afford them opportunities to take their thinking and learning deeper, to relate new learning to existing knowledge, to connect learning to the real-world, to begin to transfer their learning. At the conclusion of a lesson or unit, students proceed to more comprehensive assessments.

- *What have I learned? How can I take my learning to the next level?* Students need time and structures to bring closure to their learning, to consolidate learning and begin to set new learning goals. These are two big questions they can pose at this point to determine their level of proficiency or mastery. Students, like adults, need time for reflection if they are to integrate new learning into existing schemas and generate questions of curiosity and wonder.

SELF-QUESTIONING SKILLS FOR SELF-REGULATION

Framing self-questions as skills is an alternate approach to teaching students about self-regulation. Figure 2.2 outlines six skills (which correspond to the six stages in

FIGURE 3.2 Self-Questioning Skills for Self-Regulation

SKILL	USE WHEN	SAMPLE PROMPTS AND STEMS
Reflect to make meaning of daily learning targets.	You begin a new lesson	• What is my understanding of what I will be learning today? • How would I use my own words to explain each learning target to someone else? • Why is this important for me to learn?
Assess current knowledge related to the learning target.	You begin a new lesson	• What do I think I already know about today's learning target? • How can I find out if my preconceptions are correct? • How can I correct misconceptions or errors in thinking? • How can I connect what I will be learning to what I already know?
Select appropriate learning strategies.	Throughout the lesson	• What strategies do I possess that I might apply to this learning task? • What appears to be the most appropriate strategy to use at this point in the learning?
Monitor one's own progress during learning.	Throughout the lesson	• How do I know that I am on track in my learning? • What am I doing correctly? How do I know? • What is confusing me? What questions might I ask? • Where am I struggling? Where can I go for help? • What can I do differently next time?
Go deeper in learning.	After mastering basic knowledge and skill requirements	• What kinds of relationships can I establish between different things I am learning? • How can I connect my learning in this subject to what I'm learning in other subjects? To the real world?
Assess one's learning.	The lesson has ended	• What did I learn? • What have I not mastered yet? • What are my next steps?

the above cycle) along with related prompts and stems. Teachers can provide this chart to students as a stand-alone tool or use it in conjunction with the presentation of the preceding cycle.

MODEL QUESTION-ASKING THROUGH THINK-ALOUDS

Teacher modeling is the most powerful teacher of self-regulation questions. Think-alouds make teacher metacognitive questions and processing visible to learners who may not be familiar with this type of thinking. It is almost impossible to overuse think-alouds, particularly during the early stages of student development of metacognitive skills.

First-grade teacher Kehaulani Bohannon introduced her students to one of their daily learning targets with this think-aloud.

> When I begin or continue learning in class, I review the learning target and silently translate it into my own language. For example, as I look at today's target, "I can ask and answer questions when I investigate animal ears," I am thinking that I'll be exploring what the ears of different animals look like and maybe how they work so that these animals can hear. I'll explore by wondering about the ears of each animal, asking questions about things that puzzle me or cause me to be curious.

> I'm excited to learn about animal ears because I have a dog who doesn't always seem to listen to me. I wonder if there's something about his ears that makes it difficult for him to hear. Learning about animal ears should help me be a better friend to my dog.

As the teacher thinks aloud, she may stop occasionally and ask students if they agree with her interpretation of the learning target or if they have other ideas. When she completes her think-aloud, she may ask them what they think they'll learn that is interesting or important as they engage in the day's lesson. Later in the lesson, Kehaulani thought aloud about different strategies she might use to advance her learning.

> I believe that I will be able to look very closely at the pictures and try to notice all of the details about each animal's ears: *Where are they located? Are they large or small? Can I see inside of them, or are they covered?* I'll also need to read carefully, to look for facts describing these ears. I think it might help me to talk with classmates about what they notice, to find out if they are noticing things that I do not. As I ask questions, I'll use some of the sentence stems we've talked about. I'll try to form questions about things for which I do not know the answers. These are some of the strategies I think I will use as I begin learning about animal ears.

ADOPT ROUTINES AND PROTOCOLS

Teachers can invite students to pause, reflect, and generate questions at preplanned and strategic points in a lesson. Many teachers invite students to maintain question journals or to record questions in a designated space in their content area journals. This straight-forward and simple routine is effective. Sometimes, however, it is helpful to embed the reflection and self-questioning within a structure. Below are two examples of structures that can be used at identified points in a lesson. The first is a thinking routine that can be employed to activate student thinking about questions, or "puzzles," at any point in a lesson. The second can support question generation at the beginning, middle, or end of a lesson. These are only two of multiple structures that can be used for these purposes.

Ron Ritchhart and colleagues at Harvard's Project Zero developed what they call "thinking routines" (Ritchhart & Church, 2020; Ritchart, Church, & Morrison, 2011). Designed to make student thinking visible, these structures scaffold student thinking through the provision of prompts that elicit and focus thinking. One such routine, Think-Puzzle-Explore (TPE), is a structure that supports student metacognitive thinking better than the traditional Know–Want to Know–Learned (KWL) template that serves a similar purpose. TPE provides these three prompts to students: *What do I think I know? What puzzles me? How might we explore?* This routine can be used to help students unpack learning targets or to assess understanding of key concepts within a lesson or unit. Students are more likely to surface preconceptions because of the safety offered by the phrase "what I think I know." As a result, teachers learn about student misconceptions more frequently. The heart of this routine is the generation of questions related to puzzles. These puzzles provide a springboard and motivator for student learning. Ritchhart has found that when students use this routine repeatedly and over time, they begin to integrate the TPE questions into their thinking as they approach new learning tasks—without use of the template!

Ink Think is a response structure that can be useful in supporting student reflection and self-monitoring at multiple points in the learning cycle. Adapted from Chalk Talk, a protocol disseminated by the National School Reform Faculty (www .nsrfharmony.org), Ink Think initially engages students in silent and independent responding focused on three to four prompts. When the purpose is to generate student questions, the instruction might be to create questions one has about key concepts related to the topic of study. Following silent reflection, individuals move to a designated wall chart (minimum 3' × 4' strips of project paper prepared and posted in advance) to record their responses to one of the prompts. Working collaboratively with four to five classmates, students maintain silence as they record their own questions, review, and build on or respond to others' questions. After two minutes or so, they rotate as a group to another wall chart where they review another team's thinking about a different prompt and add their own. As students are working, the teacher rotates, taking note of prior knowledge and of any apparent misconceptions. This is an excellent way to activate prior knowledge and understandings. This protocol can also be used to invite student questions and/or responses at other key points in a unit.

Figure 3.3 presents generic stems and prompts that can be adapted for use in Ink Think at three different stages in a unit learning cycle. As you review the questions, reflect on the following: *What might be the relative benefits to students of generating these types of questions instead of answering teacher questions? What might teachers*

At the Beginning of a Unit

- Generate questions about what you think you need to know in order to better understand _____.

- Think about what you think you already know about _____. Turn these into questions that you might pose to a friend to find out if they agree or disagree with your thinking.

- What wonderings do you have about _____? What are you really interested in discovering? Express these as questions.

Midway Through a Unit

- What questions might you ask to clear up confusion or misunderstandings you still have about _____?

- If you could ask _____ (an author, a main character, a scientist, etc.) one question about _____, what might that be?

- What questions might you ask a friend to help them assess how well they are progressing toward the learning targets?

Near the End of a Unit

Think about everything you've learned in this unit.

- What are two of the most important questions your teacher might include on a test to find out if students are understanding the big ideas of this unit?

- What is the most important question that has been answered for you about _____?

- What unanswered question do you have about _____, a question you can continue to think about and perhaps explore on your own?

learn from student responses to these questions? How might silent recording on commu-nity wall charts support student learning? How might you modify one or more of these questions for use in a particular unit of study in a content area of interest?

INCORPORATE INTO DAILY LESSONS

Planning for inclusion of appropriate metacognitive processing throughout a lesson is essential. Because taking time out for student reflection and self-questioning is not a well-established routine in our classrooms, this must become a priority in les-son planning. Teachers can use the Cycle of Student Self-Questioning (Figure 2.1) when deciding the points at which to schedule time for self-questioning to move student learning forward. Each lesson needs to begin with at least a few moments for students to refocus and surface prior knowledge and questions. This is best done following the review of daily learning targets. When beginning a new unit, teachers may wish to include a routine or protocol (e.g., Ink Think) to ensure time and struc-ture for deeper thinking. Simple verbal prompts by the teacher, together with an occasional think-aloud, are sufficient for most daily lessons. Depending upon the lesson purpose, teachers can plan for students to focus on one or more of the prompts in the cycle. For example, when students are in the beginning stages of learning, teachers might pause to ask them to generate questions related to any confusions or misunderstandings. In turn, after time for development of sufficient surface knowledge, students can be prompted to pose questions focused on possible relationships between different concepts.

MAKE TIME AND SPACE

Intentional lesson planning of points in the lesson for student reflection and self-questioning is necessary but not sufficient to providing the opportunity. As previously stated, we must prioritize the metacognitive and not allow self-questioning to be the first to be "cut" when feeling the press of pacing. Establishing routine points in the lesson for the process can assist with this. At a minimum, this can be done at the beginning and end of a lesson. For example, the daily "bell-ringer" activity could consist of student generation of self-questions by reference to notes from the previous day or to the daily learning targets. In turn, the now well-established exit ticket could invite student questions related to one or more of the stages of self-regulation. Additionally, simply pausing after 10 minutes or so of direct instruction to afford time for student processing and question generation is a simple but effective technique.

AFFORD PRACTICE WITH FEEDBACK

Planning for and affording time for student reflection and self-questioning on a routine basis enables students to practice and develop this skill over time. Increased comfort and proficiency in forming their own questions will come with practice, especially when teachers provide reinforcement and feedback. During the early stages of learning, you may wish to have students record these questions in their journals so you can review and comment on the questions periodically. As with all learning tasks, specific and constructive feedback—especially questions that cause further reflection—can support improvement over time.

INVITE STUDENT REFLECTION

Consider periodic discussions with students about the value of taking time to form their questions. You might wish to pose such questions as: *In what ways does reflecting to identify questions support your learning? What about this process is challenging to you? What is supporting you as you seek to become a better self-questioner? At what points in the learning cycle do you find it most useful to pause and self-question?*

Student Questioners at Work

Students in Tracy Ray's third-grade science classroom routinely use self-questions in conjunction with learning scales to self-assess and monitor their progress. Calibrated to the district's proficiency scales, they support a standards-referenced assessment system. Mrs. Ray developed these scales in student-friendly language as the sample below, related to the third-grade weather unit, illustrates.

While students reference the proficiency scales daily to meet learning targets, Mrs. Ray plans explicit time for students to reflect on their learning after formative and summative assessments, usually midway through and at the end of each unit. These self-reflections allow students to assess where they are in their learning cycle and to set goals for class and independent learning times. As they reflect, Mts. Ray asks them: *What questions do you have about the vocabulary listed in this scale? What*

questions do you have about what we are learning in this unit? They refer to their journals, texts, and class charts to review the questions they have asked along the way and record reflections and questions on their proficiency scales.

This process prepares them for individual conferences with Mrs. Ray. The reflections and self-questions recorded on the scale allow her to clear up misconceptions, reteach as needed, and formatively assess the class for instructional next steps. Mrs. Ray notes the importance of self-questions to effective student self-assessment. She commented, "Prior to teaching students how to self-question, they seemed to think that rubrics or scales were for me. After learning how to self-question to monitor their progress towards meeting the learning targets, students began to own the process and use these tools to become leaders of their own learning." ∎

(Continued)

(Continued)

My Learning Scale

Science: Earth's Systems

Learning Target: I can display data graphically and in tables to describe typical weather conditions.

Name:

SCORE	STEPS TO SUCCESS	ACTIVITIES TO SHOW WHAT I KNOW AND GROW!
4 I can do new tricks!	❑ I can explain how weather patterns are cycles that repeat. I can use evidence to support my claim about what the weather will be like during a particular season for the following year in a local area.	What can I do to continue my learning about this topic?
3 I can do this by myself!	❑ I can identify typical weather patterns expected for a season to describe typical weather conditions during a particular season. ❑ I can represent data in tables and various graphical formats.	What can I do to continue my learning about this topic?
2 I am close!	❑ I can describe typical weather conditions expected during a particular season. ❑ I can interpret data in tables and graphs. ❑ I can learn science vocabulary: data, graphs, table, seasons, average, typical, temperature, precipitation, wind direction, Celsius, Fahrenheit.	What can I do if I need support?
1 I need support!	❑ I require support and help to identify typical weather patterns and represent and interpret weather data.	What do I need to learn?

Ways to show what I know:

❑ I can highlight items we have worked on in class in yellow; this shows what I have been taught in class and am still working on mastering.

❑ I can check off skills that I have mastered.

Developed by Tracy Ray, Third-Grade Science Teacher, DeArmanville Elementary, Oxford City Schools.

Spotlight: Online Opportunities for Self-Regulation Questions

Begin with the end in mind. The goal is for students to automatically and consistently use self-questions to monitor and adjust as they navigate a standards-driven lesson. This is particularly important for at-risk students (Fisher, Frey, & Hattie, 2020). And yet we know that many students do not currently have this capacity. How can we scaffold and support the development and use of self-regulation questions when students are working remotely? How can we use online tools to support and promote self-regulation when students are physically present with us?

Highlight the appropriate mindframe, skills, and tools for students in the lesson where particular question types will be emphasized. The operative mindframe, *I ask questions to myself to reflect on and monitor my learning,* might be appropriately positioned as a masthead on the landing page for daily lessons. This way of approaching learning needs ongoing reinforcement. Either The Cycle of Learning, Figure 3.1, or Self-Questioning Skills for Self-Regulation should be placed in a highly visible and easily accessible space.

Strategically position formal requests for student self-questions in the unit or lesson. Questions of this type are essential at the beginning and end of a lesson. A request can be as simple as prompting students to examine learning targets and generate questions they may have about the meaning of one or more. This facilitates student meaning-making and internalization of

the learning goals. Likewise, at the end of a daily lesson, students benefit from the opportunity to form and record questions that represent their next steps in their learning progression. Such questions can serve as valuable formative feedback to the teacher. In turn, at critical junctures in the lesson, students might be invited to enter questions they have about the effectiveness of strategies they are using or other questions about "how they are going" on their learning journey.

Adapt protocols and response routines for online use. An easily transferable thinking routine is Think-Puzzle-Explore, which can be effectively used, particularly at the beginning of a unit. This protocol can prompt students to think about and make meaning of learning targets, activate prior understandings, and encourage the generation of questions. Ink Think, introduced earlier in this chapter, can be used to capture student questions during a synchronous learning session. Zoom, for example, has a whiteboard on which students can record their questions and thinking.

Carefully select a limited number of tech tools (i.e., platforms and apps) for use by a class of students. Students may record questions either orally or in writing. It is helpful to provide a space where they can be archived and thereby serve as learning target trackers over time. The portfolio features of SeeSaw, ClassDojo, and like apps provide an easy way for

(Continued)

(Continued)

young learners to record questions at the beginning and end of classes and save them for future review. Older students can use Google Docs or Blogger, for example, to record written questions for archiving. In the alternative, students can be prompted to record questions in a digital journal or notebook. Tucker (2020), who emphasizes the importance of developing metacognitive skills during blended learning, describes how to use Google Sites for this purpose with secondary students (p. 136). Elementary teachers find it easier for their students to maintain physical journals for documentation of questions over time. These young students can photograph and place page(s) from their journals on a device like SeeSaw and video themselves explaining their thinking. The beauty of all of these tools is the opportunity for teachers to respond with their own questions or other feedback about the students' thinking. ∎

MAKING MEANING—DEVELOPING STUDENT CAPACITY TO ASK SELF-QUESTIONS TO BUILD UNDERSTANDING

Students use the first category of self-questions (self-regulation) to manage their learning. The second category of self-questions focuses on advancing understanding of the content or skills they are learning. Whether used for reading comprehension, problem-solving in math or science, or unraveling another academic undertaking, these questions are specific to the subject or discipline and support independent learners. They relate to individual comprehension and meaning-making.

> **A Second Student Mindframe Related to Self-Questioning:** *I ask questions to figure out the meaning of what I am reading or hearing and to think through problems and tasks.*

Many students are naturally inclined to ask themselves these types of questions. Years ago, a high school freshman who was part of a focus group on student learning was asked this question: "What supports your learning in school?" She immediately responded: "When I ask and answer questions to myself about what I am learning" (Walsh & Sattes, 2005). Many students, however, never learn the value of this process for increasing their reading comprehension or boosting their performance on other cognitive tasks. It is important to present this mindframe to students and, as with other student mindframes, allow them time to think about what this might look like, talking together about how it might support their learning. This way of thinking about approaching ones' reading or problem-solving in any area is a life skill, one that contributes to independent, lifelong learners.

While self-questions related to self-regulation are fairly generic across content areas, self-questioning to make meaning is a content-specific endeavor. As with other types of questions, students are more likely to use these effectively when they are explicitly taught. This involves teacher use of the steps highlighted earlier—including introducing strategies and stems, modeling through use of think-alouds, combining skill development with content in daily learning targets, selecting appropriate strategies, and intentional attention to the other steps.

This section provides a sampling of self-questioning strategies across core content areas. These strategies are representative but far from exhaustive. They are offered to stimulate your interest and motivate you to delve more deeply into self-questioning in your academic area(s) of focus. Students benefit from self-questions across all disciplines, including the arts, physical education, career-tech, foreign languages, and so forth. The reading comprehension strategies offered in the following section can be adapted to all of these areas. All teachers are encouraged to seek out other resources to support skill development related to their discipline or content area.

SELF-QUESTIONING TO ENHANCE READING COMPREHENSION

Elementary educators have long been familiar with the findings of the National Reading Panel. The report, released in 2000, resulted from a review of more than 100,000 studies related to reading and the improvement of student achievement (National Institute of Child Health and Human Development, 2000.) One of six powerful strategies identified by the panel is the generation of questions (or "self-questioning"). The panel recommended "explicitly teaching students to monitor their comprehension by asking and answering questions while they were reading" (p. 106).

Multiple strategies for teaching self-questioning in reading instruction have been tested and touted. Many advocate providing students with standard prompts to use while reading. For example, these four key questions were used in a study of middle schoolers focused on the benefits of active monitoring of understanding while reading: *Does that make sense? How do I know? Do I understand this? Do I understand this well enough to use in the required task?* (Israel et al., 2005, p. 143).

Figure 3.4 offers three key self-questioning skills, along with an indication of when these skills can be productively applied. These are accompanied by sample prompts and stems to share and post for students. Teachers can reproduce this template and tape it to student desks to provide a reminder and tool for students to access whenever they are reading. These skills are appropriate for readers of all ages and reading levels. Explicit teaching of these skills, clearly explaining the what, why, and when, is essential. Students will learn the skills from teacher modeling and from opportunities to practice individually and with partners and from ongoing feedback.

FIGURE 3.4 Self-Questioning Skills for Use During Silent Reading or Listening

SKILL	SAMPLE PROMPTS AND STEMS
Ask questions to yourself to make meaning of the most important facts or ideas you read or hear.	• What seems to be the most important idea? • What is confusing me? • What don't I understand? • How would I explain this in my own words?
Ask questions to connect content to what you already know.	• What comes to mind when I read (or hear) this? • What do I already know about this? • Does this contradict something I think I know? • In what ways does this add to or extend what I already know?
Ask questions that help you draw conclusions about what you are reading or hearing.	• Why might this be true? • What do I think about this? • I wonder . . . • What might have led to ____?

A more specific reading strategy relates to student posing of questions before, during, and after their reading. Such questions can vary by grade level, but variations on the following appear in most suggested lists.

FIGURE 3.5 Prompts and Stems for Use Before, During, and After Reading

BEFORE	DURING	AFTER
• What clues does the title provide about the contents of the story? • Is this an informational text or an imaginary story? • What do I already think or know about this topic? • What predictions can I make about this story?	• What does this sentence or paragraph mean to me? • Is there a word or phrase that I don't understand? How can I find out or figure out the meaning? • How can I use pictures, charts, or other visuals to help me better understand? • What picture is the author painting for me in my mind? • How would I explain what I just read to a friend? • Do I need to reread?	• Is there anything in the text that surprised me? • Which of my predictions were correct? What is my evidence? • What were the big ideas in this reading? • What did I find most interesting? • What connections can I make to what I already knew or have experienced? • What questions would I like to ask the author?

Second-grade ELA teacher Jennifer Patterson provides her students a grade-appropriate set of before, during, and after questions, along with ongoing instruction on how they might use these. She oftentimes uses the thinking routine See-Think-Wonder (Ritchhart, 2011) to scaffold student formation of the "before" questions. Mrs. Patterson has found that most second graders first need to understand what a question is and how it differs from a statement. She finds that this can be a challenge. She believes that when they are first prompted to notice and then think about parts of a text, they are better able to wonder, creating a question they want to answer. This teacher asks her students to record their questions and wonders in their journals so that they can refer to them later. Combining these three strategies—time for before, during, and after questions; use of See-Think-Wonder; and use of a question journal—Mrs. Patterson is developing her young learners' skills in self-questioning. ▪

Video 3.2: "Self-Questioning to Monitor Reading Comprehension"

SELF-QUESTIONING IN SOCIAL STUDIES CLASSROOMS

The value of self-questioning while reading extends beyond reading classrooms into all content areas and across all grade levels. One investigation of seventh-grade students found the teaching of self-questioning skills in social studies classes to improve reading comprehension and achievement (Berkeley et al., 2010). Students learned a two-part strategy, each part composed of four steps: (1) Use subheadings to create questions; (2) read the section; (3) stop; (4) attempt to answer the question. If unsure of responses, (1) reread the section; (2) double-check understanding of vocabulary; (3) review maps, graphs, or photos; (4) record questions to ask teacher. The teachers modeled through think-alouds and provided guided practice before releasing students to use the strategy independently. Standard, grade-level texts were used by all students, representing a wide ability range. Not only did the comprehension scores of participating students increase, the students stated it to be a useful strategy.

Older students can benefit from a more sophisticated type of self-questioning in the social sciences. De La Paz and Felton taught high school students how to evaluate historical documents using questions that focused on the salient features of a document, including the author's viewpoint and its reliability (De La Paz & Felton, 2010, as cited in Hattie & Yates, 2014). The researchers taught students to use both procedural and evaluative questions as they analyzed a given document or source (p. 74.) A posttest involved students reading and analyzing a different set of historical documents and writing an essay based upon their analysis. Students who learned this questioning strategy were able to transfer it to different document analyses and the writing of an essay based upon the analyses. The students displayed increased skills in primary document analysis and a greater depth of understanding of how disciplinary knowledge is generated. The explicit teaching of the skills and questions provided students with a repertoire of questions they were able to internalize and use in independent research.

SELF-QUESTIONING TO ENHANCE MATHEMATICAL PROBLEM-SOLVING

Self-questioning advances students' capacity to engage in independent, successful mathematical problem-solving (Asik et al., 2015). When students pose questions as they address a mathematical problem, they become actively engaged in thinking and testing alternate approaches. Without explicit instruction, however, most students lack the skills to engage in this process.

Way (2011) argues that many primary teachers have difficulty transferring questioning skills from literacy to mathematics and, as a result, young students do not have models for effective questioning in mathematics. She advocates explicitly teaching four different types of questions for mathematical problem-solving: (1) starter questions, (2) questions to stimulate mathematical thinking, (3) assessment questions, and (4) final discussion questions. The first three question types lend themselves to independent use by students. Figure 3.6 offers some standard prompts that teachers can use as they begin to teach students to self-question when they approach a problem.

FIGURE 3.6 Prompts for Student Self-Questions in Mathematical Problem-Solving

STARTER QUESTIONS	QUESTIONS TO STIMULATE MATHEMATICAL THINKING	ASSESSMENT QUESTIONS
• Have I seen a problem similar to this one? • How many ways can I find to . . . ? • What happens when I . . . ?	• How is this similar to . . . ? • How is this different from . . . ? • Do I see a pattern? • What comes next? What makes me think this?	• What did I discover? • Why did I decide to use the strategy I used? • Can I think of another way to do this? • Do I think I've found the best solution?

SELF-QUESTIONING TO ENGAGE
STUDENTS IN SCIENTIFIC THINKING

Self-questioning to monitor understanding and generate self-feedback supports learning in science, as in other content areas. In science, such self-questioning enhances the possibility that students will detect errors and surface misconceptions, critical to deep learning in science (Almarode et al., 2018).

Comprehension of science texts is essential to science learning. The skills required for self-questioning to increase comprehension of science texts are similar to those employed in the reading of texts in other disciplines. Science teachers can adapt those provided in Figure 2.4 to the science classroom. Slightly different stems were offered to students participating in a study focused on the impact of self-questioning on comprehension and achievement in science (Matibag-Angeles, 2016). These students received two types of question stems. The first type of stems, compulsory, included, *What was the main idea of _____? What is another example of _____? What would happen if _____?* The second group of stems given to students were these "free-choice" ones: *Explain how _____. What is the difference between _____ and _____? What conclusion can you draw about _____? How does _____ affect _____? How is _____ related to _____?* (p. 157).

The results of this study demonstrated student use of a self-questioning active reading strategy to be equally effective for low- and high-performing students. Another significant finding was that traditionally low-performing students comprehend authentic, elaborated texts when they are taught self-questioning active reading strategies and that these students' achievement levels are higher than those of their peers who read less-challenging texts. The investigator concluded that teaching low-performing students these skills can help to close the achievement gap in the learning of science.

Deep learning in science also depends upon students asking themselves questions as they "do" science in order to construct scientific understandings. One simple but effective method is to support students in developing self-questions as they engage in scientific problem-solving. By reference to traditional steps in the scientific method, students can create questions for use in scientific problem-solving, such as, *What questions might I ask to determine the cause of this problem—to create my hypothesis? What are some alternative ways to investigate this problem? What alternative methods could I use to test my hypothesis? What criteria can I use to select an alternative approach? What can I infer from the data I'm collecting?* and so on.

Alvermann (2004) discusses the importance of two types of questions identified by Chin (2001) to the learning of science: basic information questions and wonderment questions. Wonderment questions engage students in higher-level processing and include *hypothesis-verification* questions (e.g., What if I pour some water in this solution?), *anomaly* questions (e.g., How do you know that salt is in this solution?), *application* questions (e.g., What is this chemical used for?), and *plan*

> Students do not automatically ask wonderment questions. Leaving this to chance is "tantamount to letting students' puzzlements go undetected and, in effect, stifling further inquiry."

or *strategy* questions (e.g., What are we going to do next?). Students do not automatically ask wonderment questions. Leaving this to chance is "tantamount to letting students' puzzlements go undetected and, in effect, stifling further inquiry" (p. 13). Explicit teaching of self-questioning skills is essential in science, as in other content areas. Scaffolding student development of self-questioning skills is key to helping them think like scientists.

In Closing: *Changing the Equation*

Many students depend upon their teachers to direct their learning—to tell them what strategy to use, to assess their progress, to provide feedback, and to evaluate their learning. Developing student capacity to self-question can facilitate the metacognitive functioning required to put students in charge of their own learning. Hattie and Donoghue (2016) describe self-regulation "as the interplay of the will to invest in learning, curiosity and willingness to explore what one does not know, and the skills to pursue a deeper understanding of content" (The National Academies of Sciences-Engineering-Medicine, 2018, p. 73). By continually facilitating students' *skill, will, and thrill* related to self-questioning metacognitively, teachers can help change the responsibility equation.

Begin with the end in mind. Self-questions to make personal meaning take on heightened importance in an online environment. These types of questions support comprehension, application, and analysis during reading, problem-solving, and other self-paced learning tasks. Developing and supporting this set of metacognitive skills is a challenging but high-yield teaching strategy.

Highlight the appropriate mindframe, skills, and tools for students in the lesson where a particular question type will be emphasized. Given the importance of this metacognitive skill to student success when working independently, time invested in reviewing and modeling the mindframe and related skills during synchronous learning is well spent. Remind students of what this mindframe looks and sounds like in action: *I ask questions to figure out the meaning of what I am reading or hearing and to think through problems and tasks.* Focus on the skills and sample prompts in Table 3.4. This is important not only for elementary reading instruction but as illustrated in this chapter, for learning in all content areas.

Strategically position formal requests for student self-questions in the unit or lesson. As with self-regulation questions, the vision is for meaning-making questions to become ubiquitous, to permeate each student's approach to self-paced work. Cueing students to use this type of question is critical as you make an assignment that involves sustained self-paced work.

Adapt protocols and response routines for online use. Structures for student notetaking during independent work are helpful scaffolds. A simple two-column template, "Insights" and "Questions," provides a space for students to record big ideas and questions that emerge from a reading. You can create subject-specific question-capturing templates by reference to Figure 3.6 (self-questions in math) as well as for the prompts offered for learning in science.

Carefully select a limited number of tech tools (i.e., platforms and apps) for use by a class of students. Self-questions are, as the name suggests, personal and private, supporting independent reading, processing, and learning. To scaffold their use, however, teachers can build in periodic opportunities for students to reflect on their success in using such questions and to receive feedback from their teacher. Platforms that support oral student responding include Flipgrid for all age groups and SeeSaw and ClassDojo, especially for younger students. The value of the teacher modeling the use of these through think-alouds cannot be overemphasized. Time dedicated to this during synchronous sessions (via Zoom, Google Meet, or another selected platform) can pay significant dividends in student learning outcomes.

Curtain Call: Revisiting Key Ideas

KEY IDEAS	QUESTIONS FOR PERSONAL REFLECTION
1. Self-questions are the drivers of student self-regulation and meaning-making. The expectation is that students become deliberate and intentional in questioning themselves to monitor progress toward learning goals and to check their understanding of written text, auditory input, and other external stimuli.	• What practices are you currently using intentionally and consistently to develop self-questioning skills in your students? • Given the developmental level of your students and the grade and content areas you teach, in what ways do you believe your students might directly benefit from becoming more confident and capable self-questioners?
2. Student Mindframes: *I ask myself questions to regulate my thinking and learning and to promote comprehension and problem-solving,* and *I ask questions to figure out the meaning of what I am reading or hearing and to think through problems and tasks.*	• To what extent are your students currently aware of the value of engaging in metacognitive practices? • How might you help your students unpack these mindframes to understand what they mean and how they might affect their way of engaging with their academic tasks?
3. The Cycle of Student Learning and Thinking is a tool for students to use in self-regulating their learning. It specifies six questions that students can use as they move through a given learning task.	• In what ways might this tool be used by your students, given their developmental level and the discipline(s) you teach? • How might you introduce this tool to your students? How might you maintain their focus on the process over time?
4. Students benefit when their teachers think aloud about their metacognitive processing and provide guided practice in using questions to advance this type of thinking.	• At what specific points in instruction might you model self-questioning through surfacing and articulating your thinking to your students? • What kinds of visual cues might you use to connect students with key questions and processes?
5. Most students do not automatically engage in self-regulation; teachers must make time and space for this to occur within daily instruction.	• Imagine that you are developing a lesson plan for a selected class. At what points might you incorporate opportunities for reflection to self-regulate? What scaffolds or tools could you provide to support students in the process? • Can you imagine making time for such self-regulation a routine or regular feature of all lesson plans? What might be the benefits? The challenges?
6. Teaching students how to use self-questions while reading, problem-solving, and engaging in other academic tasks enhances their performance.	• Which of the stems for use by students to make meaning while working independently do you find most useful? • How might you go about introducing this process and related stems to your students?

CHAPTER 4

Academic Questions
Clarifying and Deepening Understanding

I pose questions to clarify and deepen my understanding of academic content.

Student Questioners at Work

Students in Jarid Moore's geometry class are harnessing the power of questions to transfer geometric understandings to real-world applications. These students move comfortably from individual reflection to small-group dialogue to whole-class discussion. At each turn, they pose questions to one another and use these questions to forge deeper understandings. During this videotaped lesson, learners begin by listening to a designated partner's explanation of a problem and posing questions to get behind and sometimes challenge their peer's thinking. Following a brief presentation by their teacher, they reflect silently to form a question about a new problem and then move to examine their partner's question. Pairs combine to form quads where questions are shared and compared and one is selected for beginning dialogue. The lesson culminates with whole group sharing of insights emerging from the quad conversations. Mr. Moore's lesson design capitalizes on student questions and collaborative learning and enables students to reinforce surface knowledge, deepen understandings as they find relationships between different concepts, and transfer learning to new settings. ■

Video 4.1: "Student Questions Propel Learning of Geometry"

Academic questions advance student understanding of content and mastery of standards. In traditional teacher-centered classrooms, teachers are almost always the questioners; students, usually the passive respondents. The primary premise of this chapter is straightforward: When teachers provide students with the tools, the time, and the learning focus required to conceptualize and ask productive questions, students become more engaged, successful learners. In effect, students are no longer simply an audience for teacher performances; they become active contributors to a community of learners.

In classrooms where students form a community of learners, teachers do not abdicate their responsibility for structuring or designing lessons or for guiding learning. They provide students with learning goals and success criteria that clearly communicate the expectations for learning. These enable students to have clarity regarding their learning destination and to use self-questions to monitor their progress. They also serve to anchor student thinking that leads them to form questions about what they need to know (surface knowledge), relationships between and among different concepts (deep knowledge), and how they might apply learning in new, ideally real-world, settings (transfer knowledge.) Academic questions span these three phases of learning.

BUILDING A KNOWLEDGE BASE—DEVELOPING STUDENT CAPACITY TO ASK ACADEMIC QUESTIONS

Students encounter countless academic questions as they move through the days, weeks, months, and years of schooling. Teachers ask them orally and in writing, face-to-face, and electronically; textbook chapters and workbooks are replete with these; and assessments at all levels—from classroom to college admissions—are composed of these types of questions. Students who are good at answering such questions excel at the game of school. Too many of our students can neither interpret the questions nor provide expected answers; they are labeled failures.

All students benefit from forming their own questions related to learning goals. Those who have been largely unable to answer other people's questions have the most to gain. All students have latent questions. Most do not have *the will* to ask because they do not believe this to be their role. Underachieving students often lack both the will and the skill to question.

> "In the traditional classroom, students are perceived as relatively passive learners who receive wisdom from teachers, textbooks, or other media. In the community of learners classroom, students are encouraged to engage in self-reflective learning and critical inquiry. They act as researchers who are responsible, to some extent, for defining their own knowledge and expertise. In the community of learners classroom, teachers are expected to serve as active role models of learning and as responsive guides to students' discovery processes."—Brown and Campione, 1998, p. 153.

Begin With the Mindframe. *I form and ask questions to clarify and deepen my understanding of academic content.*

As with other mindframes, "I" is the subject and the first word of this statement. As you introduce your students to this way of viewing their role as learners, invite them to reflect on these questions: *How often do I ask questions to clarify confusion I may be experiencing during learning? When am I most likely to ask such questions publicly? Whom do I ask?* Instruct them to turn and exchange their responses with a partner and be ready to share out with the whole group. During group sharing, seek to understand your students' perspectives. As their conversation continues, gently ask them, *What keeps you from voicing your questions out loud in class?* Next, challenge students to generate benefits to them individually and to their classmates that might result from their assuming the role of questioners. Finally, ask, *What can I and other teachers do to support you in accepting the responsibility of questioning to clarify?*

Embedding the mindframe and related skills in daily learning targets reinforces expectations for questioning. For example, in the videotaped class featured in

Video 4.2, U.S. history teacher Adam Clark calls student attention to the following target: "I can ask questions to discuss the controversial events that led to the worsening of events in Europe following WWI." After a student reads and comments on this learning goal, Mr. Clark engages the class in thinking about the importance of asking the right question to get to the root of an issue. He illustrates this point by showing a short clip from the Will Smith movie *I, Robot* (Proyas, 2004), in which Smith's character, Del Spooner, questions a hologram to uncover clues in a case. Following the viewing, students think about why it is important to persist in asking follow-up questions to get the information needed. Mr. Clark then reviews the characteristics of a quality question with the students and provides them time to assess their previously prepared focus questions to make any last-minute revisions. Facilitating student reflection on the why and how of question-asking on a routine basis can help strengthen this new habit.

TEACHING STRATEGIES AND SKILLS

Continuing to focus on this mindframe as you move forward strengthens efforts to shift responsibility for asking questions to the learners. At appropriate points in time, initiate discussions about what is involved in "deepening" understanding. Assist students in sharing their understanding of the primary differences between *surface* and *deep* knowledge.

Hattie substitutes the term *reproductive performance* for surface learning and notes, "Surface learning includes subject matter vocabulary, the content of the lesson, and knowing much more" (Hattie & Donoghue, 2016, p. 3). Surface learning is not to be confused with superficial learning. It is not mere memorization of facts. Rather, surface learning supports students in developing a conceptual understanding of ideas, skills, or procedures sufficient to connect the new learning to other concepts and later draw upon and use this knowledge to problem solve, create, and engage in other higher cognitive tasks (Hattie & Zierer, 2017). As you help students understand surface knowledge, you may begin to tease out some of the benefits of asking clarifying questions as they begin learning a new concept.

Provide students with a simple definition of deep learning to allow them to distinguish it from surface learning. Emphasize that when they engage in deep learning, they will begin to make connections between two different ideas, to develop linkages between and among different concepts (e.g., by comparing and contrasting, looking for cause-and-effect relationships, etc.).

It is helpful to return to this mindframe as students engage in a learning journey that moves them from surface to deep understandings and, as described in the next section, assists them in using this understanding in conceptualizing questions that will advance their own learning and support that of their peers.

As students come to understand how questions vary at different points in learning, they can benefit from a list of generic questions and stems. Starter words help students of all ages reflect on what they might need to know to take the next step in learning. The tables that follow offer a beginning set of skills and prompts teachers can modify to fit the developmental level of their students and the particular needs of their discipline or content area. After customizing these tables, many teachers miniaturize and tape these to student desks.

Questions to Build Surface Understandings. These questions emerge from student reflection that arises from metacognitive processing (described in the previous chapter). When learners use learning goals and success criteria to self-assess, they become aware of their basic "needs to know" if they are to move their learning forward. The template appearing as Figure 4.1 is a tool for use by students as they move from self-assessing, through conceptualizing their questions, to asking these of their teacher or a peer.

FIGURE 4.1 Skills and Stems to Support Surface Learning

SKILL	USE WHEN	SAMPLE PROMPTS AND STEMS
Ask questions to clarify something that doesn't make sense to you.	• You don't know the meaning of a word or phrase. • You are confused by wording or sentence structure. • What you read or hear differs from what you thought you knew.	• How are you defining _____? • What did the author mean when she wrote _____? • What do you mean when you say . . . ? • I thought _____. Is this incorrect? • How would you summarize _____?
Ask questions to better understand the meaning of a topic or text.	• You would like an example. • You would like to hear another way of explaining this.	• Can you give me an example of _____? • Can you say this in another way? • I understand _____ to mean _____. Is this a correct way of thinking about this topic?
Pose questions to learn more about a topic.	• You would like to know more about a subject or topic.	• Where might I learn more about this? • Would you elaborate on _____? • Would you say more about _____?
Find out if you have a complete understanding of something.	• You would like to know if you have a complete understanding of an idea.	• I'm not clear about how you reached this answer (or conclusion). Will you go through the steps once more? • This is what I'm thinking: _____. What have I left out?

> Empowering students as questioners enables them to move more seamlessly across the different levels of learning.

Questions to Develop Deep Learning. Movement from surface to deep to transfer learning does not always occur in a linear fashion. Students may move back and forth, especially when given freedom to manage their own learning. Student readiness to pursue deep understandings occurs at different points in the curriculum and at different times from student to student. Empowering students as questioners enables them to move more seamlessly across the different levels of learning. This enhances engagement and allows for self-differentiation in learning. Information provided in Figure 4.2 can support students' bridging from surface to deep.

> *Why do I need to know this?* can be the most powerful of all student questions because it can serve to nurture interest and inspire deeper learning.

Questions That Support Transfer Learning. Encouraging students to imagine how academic concepts and skills can be utilized to solve real problems or create new designs feeds motivation and engagement. The intersection of deep knowing with an opportunity to use the knowledge in a novel manner contributes to *the thrill* of learning. As students are drawn into this level of learning, they are able to reinforce surface knowledge (by further consolidating understandings) and deepen knowledge (for example, by investigating possible relationships). *Why do I need to know this?* can

FIGURE 4.2   Skills and Stems to Support Deep Learning

SKILL	USE WHEN	SAMPLE PROMPTS AND STEMS
Ask questions to understand the relationship between two different things.	• You wonder how one thing is like (or different from) another. • You wonder whether one thing might have caused another.	• How is _____ similar to _____? • How is _____ different from _____? • What do _____ and _____ have in common? • What may have contributed to _____? • What resulted from _____? • What effect would that have? • What might have caused this?
Inquire about the importance or value of something.	• You are trying to decide why something is important. • You are attempting to evaluate or assess the relative importance of a person, event, or thing.	• How will I be able to use this? • How will this help me _____? • What makes this important _____? • How might we go about evaluating _____? • What criteria (or standards) can we use to judge _____?

be the most powerful of all student questions because it can serve to nurture interest and inspire deeper learning. The sample prompts and stems in Figure 4.3 are a simple "starter kit" for instigating student thinking about possibilities for transfer. Transfer questions can generate sparks that fire student imagination and transport them to the realm of curiosity and exploration that will be the focus of Chapter 5.

FIGURE 4.3   Skills and Stems to Support Transfer Learning

SKILL	USE WHEN	SAMPLE PROMPTS AND STEMS
Ask questions to determine how something might work in the real world.	• You wonder how something might help solve a real-world problem. • You are trying to decide if a principle or idea has any practical value.	• Could we use this to _____? • What challenges might we face if we tried to use this to _____? • How might _____ affect a decision to _____?
Inquire into what might happen if an idea, principle, or event occurred in a different context.	• You wonder what might happen if you changed one variable or part of a principle, rule, or concept. • You want to adapt something to work in a different setting.	• What might we need to consider if we used this to _____? • What if we changed _____? Would we be able to use this to _____? • What if _____ happened? How would that affect _____? • What could get in the way of _____ working?

Criteria for Developing and Assessing Quality Questions. During the early stages of learning to conceptualize and form their own questions, students benefit from understanding what makes a question an effective one. The success criteria presented in Figure 4.4 serve as a tool students can use to assess the quality of questions they create. The criteria address both the value of a question to student learning as well as its clarity. The criteria are generic and can be adapted for use with students in all grade levels and content areas. Learners develop facility in forming questions when they have multiple opportunities to use these in reflecting on their own questions and in providing feedback to peers.

FIGURE 4.4   Criteria for a Student-Created Academic Question

✓ *Makes you think*. Requires more than a simple yes/no or two-to-three word response. Helps clarify or extend thinking and learning.

✓ *Advances progress toward a learning target*. Relates to a learning goal or target and moves you along a proficiency scale.

✓ *Seems important*. Addresses a topic that is worth thinking about and remembering.

✓ *Is interesting*. Relates to an engaging idea or makes a real-world connection.

✓ *Is understandable*. Clearly communicates to others.

Some readers will be familiar with the work of The Right Question Institute, an organization dedicated to improving the questioning of both adults and students. *Make Just One Change: Teach Students to Ask Their Own Questions* (Rothstein & Santana, 2011) describes a multistepped process that teachers can use to assist students in generating, refining, and selecting questions that support learning.

MODEL QUESTION-ASKING THROUGH THINK-ALOUDS

Teachers who value questions for learning prepare a limited number of focus questions as a part of lesson planning. These quality questions meet certain criteria, including the following:

- Alignment with daily learning targets

- Advancement of a specific instructional purpose (e.g., activation of prior knowledge, deepening understanding of a key concept, etc.)

- Activation of student cognitive processing at the highest appropriate level

- Wording and phrasing that is clear and concise (i.e., understandable to students) (Walsh & Sattes, 2017)

> When teacher questions are carefully conceptualized and formulated, they serve as models for student questions.

When teacher questions are carefully conceptualized and formulated, they serve as models for student questions. When asking such a question in class, sharing aloud with students the thinking behind the creation of the question can promote student understanding of what they might do when formulating a question of their own.

ADOPT ROUTINES AND PROTOCOLS

If students are to ask deep questions about complex academic content, they need time and structures to develop and express their wonderings. Additionally, questioners require a setting and a set of supportive procedures for engagement of others in the investigative process. Routines and protocols scaffold student thinking as they put on their questioning hats.

Protocols provide individuals and groups with step-by-step procedures for completing a process, oftentimes a structured way of participating in a dialogue. Numbers of protocols that can be used to support students as they form and ask questions are featured throughout this book. Many are illustrated in the videotaped lessons accessible through QR codes. One of the simplest is IQ Pairs described below.

IQ Pairs

Purpose: The Insight–Question (IQ) routine engages students in pairs to talk about a short reading, quote, or question. This strategy prepares students for a large-group discussion by giving them an opportunity to identify and clarify their thoughts in a low-risk environment (pairs) before sharing in a larger group setting.

Preparation: Identify a short, thought-provoking passage, quote, or question. Have each student find a partner with whom to talk.

Facilitation: Display the passage, quote, or question so that all students can read it. Explain that after they read it, each student should share with his or her partner (1) an *insight* and (2) a *question* based on the passage. Have students record their insights on one color of sticky note and their questions on another.

After sufficient time for sharing in pairs, call on a student to report her partner's question; request several other partners share thinking before moving to whole-class discussion. Post the questions on a wall space clustering like questions together. Repeat process for insights. Use selected questions to focus a class discussion.

The Project Zero thinking routines introduced in Chapter 3 can serve as powerful scaffolds for supporting student formulation of questions. These structures, many of which are appropriate for all grade levels and content areas, are intended for routine use so that they become a way of doing business in the classroom as well as embedded patterns for student cognitive processing. Among those that are particularly useful in sparking academic questions are Think-Puzzle-Explore (described in the previous chapter) and See-Think-Wonder (featured in Video 3.2.)

I recommend selecting a limited number of routines—those most appropriate to one's discipline and student developmental level. Repeated use of two to four strategies is more likely to result in students internalizing and incorporating these approaches than use of many in the name of novelty. When students repeatedly use a routine, it can become a lens through which they engage with their world and with one with another.

Student Questioners at Work

Students in Adam Clark's U.S. history class are grappling with the aftermath of World War I. More specifically, they are delving into

(Continued)

(Continued)

Woodrow Wilson's 14 Points, the Treaty of Versailles, and the League of Nations. In previous classes, pairs of students worked together to examine one of these documents and create questions to pose to their classmates. They used criteria for quality questions to vet their questions. Mr. Clark challenged them to create questions that would stimulate thinking, deepen learning, and prompt discussion. During this lesson, he selected Inside-Outside Circles as the response structure and is using a protocol that includes an empty chair in the inside circle for listeners to occupy when they have a question or comment.

Following the class, Mr. Clark reflects to identify what went well and what he'd like to rethink for the next such lesson. Looking back, he identified occasions when some students' questions revealed inadequate surface knowledge to respond to a complex question, and he determined to think more about how he might scaffold in advance. He also noted a number of unexpected connections made by students whose depth of knowledge was impressive. In balance, he believes that releasing control to students, allowing them to grapple and support one another, is resulting in more learning than was occurring when he dished information out to them through lectures. ∎

Video 4.2:
"Student Questions Drive Learning in U.S. History"

Project Zero's Thinking Routines Toolbox. This online resource, http://pz.harvard.edu/thinking-routines, organizes dozens of thinking routines into nine categories. The user-friendly documentation of each routine describes its purpose and offers potential applications and tips for getting started.

The site is dynamic and ever-changing, as the Harvard research team adds new routines emerging from ongoing research.

Incorporate Into Daily Lessons. Academic questions are the lifeblood of classroom learning. As noted earlier, teachers typically ask dozens across a school day while students ask almost none. Planning ahead for inclusion of student questions in a class is a prerequisite to changing this imbalance. This can be as simple as assigning students the task of developing questions about a reading assignment instead of asking them to answer questions at the end of a chapter or on a worksheet. Round-Robin Questioning, described below, is a protocol that incorporates this strategy.

Round-Robin Questioning

Purpose: Gives students practice in writing and posing quality questions, using think times, and providing verbal prompts to peers, as appropriate.

Preparation: As part of a reading assignment, ask students to create five questions about the reading: four questions for which they have an idea of the answer and one question for which they believe there is no one correct answer (i.e., a true question). Initially, this can be done in collaborative groups to support students who might have initial difficulty accomplishing this task.

Facilitation: Begin by explaining the process to students. Then name one student to lead off asking one of her questions. That student poses a question; waits for three to five seconds; and names a classmate to respond, waiting again for three to five seconds to afford all time to think. If the answer is correct, the student should acknowledge it.

If the questioner does not believe the response to be correct, she elicits more information by asking questions such as *What makes you say that? How did you arrive at your answer?* or *Can you say more?* If the response is clearly incorrect, the student either provides cues (e.g., *If you look on page 36, in the first paragraph, you will see what the character was after*) or informs the responder of the incorrectness and names another student to answer.

When the first questioning episode is concluded, the responding student will pose one of his questions, wait three to five seconds, and call on a different student to respond, following the same sequence as above. This should continue until most important facts or understandings have been asked about.

The teacher should be an active listener, intervening only to facilitate management or correct misunderstandings or errors.■

As with any learning task, asking students to write questions as ends unto themselves is not good practice. Rather, plan to engage students in forming questions at points in a lesson when reflection to identify areas of confusion or wondering serve the instructional purpose.

MAKE TIME AND SPACE

Designing tasks that require students to form and write questions can support many academic outcomes. More important than the student questions that emerge from the formalized opportunities to ask, however, may be the ones that come to learners as they listen to a teacher's or a peer's explanation and experience either confusion or a eureka moment that leads to a wondering. Pacing in traditional classrooms is so hurried that students oftentimes lack the time to form these questions or to obtain recognition to ask them. As discussed in Chapter 1, intentional use of Think Times 1 and 2 can provide these openings, especially when students use the pauses for metacognitive reflection outlined in Figures 1.2 and 1.3.

The other variable affecting student willingness to ask when confused or curious is the culture embedded in the classroom learning community. Addressed in Chapter 2, the psychologically safe classroom encourages and nourishes student questions. Language, an important component of culture, also contributes to students' perceptions of the value of their questions. For example, consider the different message conveyed when a teacher asks, "What kinds of questions do you have?" instead of the more common, "Are there any questions?" Also, think about the value of a teacher's appreciative feedback in encouraging students to take risks associated with the asking of questions: "Juan's question helped me better get behind what the author may have been thinking." "I had been wondering the same thing as Shamika but was having difficulty putting my wondering into words." "Today's lesson has been so enlivened by the questions you have asked." "Your questions have really made me think more about what made this character tick."

Afford Practice With Feedback. The Criteria for Student-Created Academic Questions (Figure 4.4) supports student thinking as they develop questions. These simple criteria can also provide a basis for self-assessment and feedback by both teacher and peers. Peer feedback works best when students are provided a structure, such as the one selected by Cade Somers for his tenth-grade English students (Video 4.3). Mr. Somers chose the Praise-Question-Polish protocol for student use in offering feedback to one another. Figure 4.5 includes suggestions and prompts to support students working with this structure.

Student Questioners at Work

Cade Somers's tenth graders are preparing to conduct research related to the writing of an argumentative essay. In preparation for this task, Mr. Somers is scaffolding their development of questions to guide the research and writing. He believes that tenth graders need support and practice in forming good questions. He has selected Praise-Question-Polish (PQP), a process for structuring feedback, as a tool for his students to use in reflecting on their own and their peers' questions and providing feedback. ∎

Video 4.3: "Peer Feedback Using Praise-Question-Polish"

FIGURE 4.5   Praise-Question-Polish

Praise: Provide evidence-based feedback that addresses specific features of your peer's thinking or work product. Praise should be *contingent*, related to expected success criteria or to valued outcomes.

Question: Pose clarifying and/or eliciting questions. These questions help you better understand and get behind the thinking of your partner. *Example*s include

- *Help me understand _____.*
- *Why did you decide to _____?*
- *Which criteria did you consider as you formed _____?*
- *What assumptions are you making about _____?*
- *What do you mean when you say _____?*

Polish: Ask questions that will promote the author's reflection about his/her thinking and/or work product. The purpose of these questions is to help your partner think about how s/he might improve the quality of the work. *Example*s include

- *What if you _____?*
- *In what ways might you _____?*
- *How could you _____?*
- *What would it take to _____?*
- *Imagine that _____.*

INVITE STUDENT REFLECTION

For students, as for adults, the importance of taking time out to reflect on how a process is going cannot be overstated. Because data enhance reflection, teachers may wish to select one of the following strategies for classroom data collection to support community reflection.

- Periodically designate one student to keep a tally of the number of student questions and the number of teacher questions asked over the course of several classes. Summarize these data and create a table for display to class. Engage students in dialogue to talk about the meaning of the data and to speculate about reasons for the distribution. Archive the data and have students look for patterns over time.

- Plan to videotape 10 to 15 minutes of a lesson during which you expect and nurture student questions. Play back the video to the class and ask them to reflect on the quality and value of their questions. Provide students with a two-column note-taking sheet to use as a viewing guide. Head one column "Noticings" and the other "Wonderings." At the end of their viewing, have students compare observations to those of a partner preparatory to sharing out with the whole.

In Closing: *Changing the Equation*

Widespread consensus exists as to the usual roles for teachers and students while engaged in classroom questioning. Teachers direct the learning and ask questions. Students are actors who comply with teacher directions and answer questions. The classroom is the stage for these academic interactions. Changing the balance of power and routinized behaviors will not occur by wishing it so.

The mindframes and structures offered in this chapter can provide the architecture to shape new roles and accompanying responsibilities for academic interactions. As students learn how better to form and ask questions and come to believe that their questions matter, the balance of power and talk in classrooms will change. When students become proficient questioners, they will begin to lead their own learning—increasing their skill, stiffening their will, and experiencing the thrill that will equip them to engage in independent, life-long adventures in learning.

> As students learn how better to form and ask questions and come to believe that their questions matter, the balance of power and talk in classrooms will change.

Spotlight: Online Opportunities for Academic Questions

Begin with the end in mind. Academic questions can express a student's need for clarification of a concept or skill or interest in learning more about a topic. They are vehicles for engagement and ownership no less online than in face-to-face venues. These can be either spontaneous or prompted; posed either publicly during a synchronous session or during asynchronous learning via a medium offered by the teacher. While spontaneous and unprompted academic questions are highly valued, student questions are not always easily insertable in online environments. As a result, it is prudent to identify junctures in a lesson where they might be naturally elicited and plan prompts and structures to facilitate student asking.

Highlight the appropriate mindframe, skills, and tools for students in the lesson where particular question types will be emphasized. Students benefit from frequent reminders of the mindframe, *I form and ask questions to clarify and deepen my understanding of academic content.* Likewise, Figures 4.1, 4.2, and 4.3 (stems to support asking of questions in pursuit of surface, deep, and transfer learning) are important tools to make easily accessible to students in the online format. Find a student-friendly space on your LMS (learning management system) to place these tools. Consider including the criteria for quality academic questions, Figure 4.4, in this same location.

Strategically position formal requests for academic questions in the unit or lesson.

Eliciting student questions at different stages in learning stimulates movement from surface to deep to transfer. Consider designing independent tasks that prompt students to form their own questions for the various levels of learning rather than asking them to respond to yours. This works whenever you want students to engage in active processing of the content. Once formed and vetted, students can ask their questions to one another. Teacher questions can augment when needed.

Adapt protocols and response routines for online use. Almost all protocols can be adapted for online use, some to prepare students for participation in dialogue during synchronous sessions, others to structure their thinking and questioning while self-pacing their learning. Both protocols featured in this chapter, I-Q Pairs and Round-Robin Questioning, can be customized for online use. Both support student preparation of questions during self-paced learning and yield questions they can bring to synchronous sessions for posing to peers. Whether in breakout rooms in Zoom, Google Meet, or Microsoft Teams or on a discussion board in Schoology, Google Classroom, or another LMS, students can ask and answer one another's questions thereby contributing to ownership and community.

Carefully select a limited number of tech tools (i.e., platforms and apps) for use by a class of students. Flipgrid is a versatile app that is ideal for student asking of questions for response by peers. Appropriate for all

(Continued)

(Continued)

grade levels, it provides space for authentic questioning and responding. Padlet and Google Jamboard are apps that enable students to write their questions on notes that can be moved to form categories of like items. Mentimeter is another app that allows students to enter questions in an open-ended format for public viewing. These response structures facilitate student interaction with content and with one another.

Adam Clark, high school history and government teacher, uses apps that allow students to record their voices for both their teacher and classmates to hear. Mr. Clark believes that the voice recordings afford personalization amidst a stream of online written responses. He frequently instructs students to use VoiceThread to comment on primary documents; for example, he has instructed students to insert questions using this tool at

identified points within the Declaration of Independence. Talk&Comment and Kaizer are Microsoft extensions that can be used similarly. Vocaroo, another voice-recordin app, allows students to create a URL that others can use to access their questions a comments. Mr. Clark also employs Voxer, a walkie-talkie type app, for students to exchange questions and responses.

Tracy Ray, elementary science teacher, uses Pear Deck to solicit questions from her students as they view slides designed to offer explicit instruction during a lesson This enables her to have students pause to enter a question that both she and their classmates can view. A similar strategy of viewing and stopping for responses is effective for video viewing as well. Hattie research found interactive videos to have effect size of $d = 0.54$, among the highest distance learning (Fisher et al., p. 5). ▪

Curtain Call: Revisiting Key Ideas

KEY IDEAS	QUESTIONS FOR PERSONAL REFLECTION
1. Asking academic questions can help students clear up confusion, seek missing parts in the learning puzzle, and deepen understandings.	• How often do students in your classroom or school proactively ask questions to clarify and/or deepen understandings? • What is your reaction to the idea that student motivation and achievement can increase when they are provided opportunities to form their own academic questions?
2. Academic questions vary depending upon the level of knowledge being developed: surface, deep, and transfer knowledge.	• What might be the benefits of teaching students the nature of surface, deep, and transfer learning? • How might you use the three charts (Figure 4.2, 4.3, and 4.4) to support your students in asking these three kinds of academic questions?
3. When teachers thoughtfully and strategically plan focus questions in advance of class, they can model for students by sharing with them the thinking behind their questions.	• What is your response to the proposal that teachers plan a limited number of focus questions in advance of class that might serve as exemplars for students? • How might students benefit from teachers sharing the thinking behind their formation of questions?
4. Thinking routines and protocols are resources teachers can use when designing lessons that incorporate student questioning of one another.	• Which of the thinking routines and protocols featured in the narrative and in the videos of this chapter are you most interested in exploring with your students? • What other thinking routines and/or protocols are you and/or your colleagues using that might support student questioning-asking?
5. Regular opportunities for students to provide feedback to one another about the quality of their questions contributes to improvements over time.	• How might you use the Criteria for Student-Created Quality Questions (Figure 4.1) and/or The Questioning Continuum (featured in Video 4.3) with your students? • What benefits do you believe students might derive from reviewing one another's questions and giving and receiving feedback on their quality?

CHAPTER 5

Exploratory Questions
Expressing Wonderings and Curiosities

I use questions to channel
my curiosity and spark
my creativity.

STUDENT MINDFRAME

Meredith Barkley's biology students are beginning a unit on cell communications. One of the learning targets for the day's lesson is: "I can develop exploratory questions related to homeostasis and cell communications." Mrs. Barkley's purpose is to pique student curiosity related to these important concepts. She structures two learning experiences for her students to accomplish this end. The first strategy, designated as "Pathway with Friends," challenges teams of six students to model cell communications by physically arranging themselves in what they believe to be the correct sequence of steps. This is followed by a lab during which students dissolve miracle berries in their mouths and then taste a variety of foods. Their task is to observe how the berry affects them and to generate as many exploratory questions as possible to lead them into this unit of study. Key moments from this lesson are captured in Video 5.1, "Stimulating Curiosity and Exploratory Questions in a Biology Class."∎

Exploratory questions are questions that result from student wondering, from deep curiosity. In the classroom, they can emerge from opportunities to reflect and form self-questions and may arise from academic questions. Though related to our two previous question types, they constitute a particular category of question. Exploratory questions, as defined here, are characterized by a spirit of excitement, adventure, and discovery. They motivate students to engage in learning a particular concept or topic.

"If learning consists of exploring and making sense of things, then questioning is the call to action that ignites learning."—Wendy Ostroff, 2016, p. 86.

To qualify as exploratory, a question must be borne of curiosity. Curiosity is the subject of a large body of research and writing (e.g., Barell, 2003; Berger, 2020; Engel, 2015; Goodwin, 2020; Leslie, 2004; Livio, 2017; Ostroff, 2012, 2016). One emergent theme is the stifling of curiosity by formal education. Based on her own and others' research, Engel notes, "though children are curious, students are not" (p. 89). Almost all of these thought leaders agree that a supportive culture is prerequisite to reversing this situation and unleashing curiosity. Goodwin (2018), for example, argues that "curiosity isn't taught or compelled but, rather, emerges like a sprouting plant when conditions are right" (p. 19).

The cultivation of curiosity around academic content precedes the actual forming and posing of exploratory questions. Students must first be curious about the content they are to study. Curiosity is necessary but not sufficient to the asking of these questions. Learners must also have the capacity to form the questions and the courage to ask them aloud in a class culture where wondering and not knowing are valued (Engel, 2015).

Teachers, of course, are the shapers of this culture. Both our values and behaviors contribute to the fertile ground from which curiosity and attendant questions sprout. When we model personal curiosity by posing our own wonderings, our *"what ifs"* and *"why nots,"* we convey a willingness to think beyond the two covers of a text and an excitement about exploring new ideas. Routine expressions of curiosity communicate to our students that we value not knowing and the questions it spawns. Student curiosity blossoms in classroom cultures where questions, not answers, and doubt, not certainty, are welcomed and celebrated. Enthusiasm and passion for exploring and learning are also important in cultivating a classroom culture in which curiosity blooms.

> Student curiosity blossoms in classroom cultures where questions, not answers, and doubt, not certainty, are welcomed and celebrated.

Teachers can ignite student curiosity by designing experiences that stimulate wondering (Engel & Labella, 2011; Ostroff, 2012). Knowledge gaps are primary catalysts for curiosity, particularly when students see the relevance of the gap and feel empowered to close it (Hattie & Yates, 2014, p. 7). To facilitate the conversion of curiosities to questions, teachers provide time and structures that enable students to capture the curiosities in written form. Mrs. Barkley constructed the miracle berry lab to ignite curiosity; she offered time and scaffolds for each student to form and share questions growing out of the experience.

Explorations borne of curiosity yield multiple benefits, including increased engagement and deeper learning. Researchers associate the activation of curiosity with

✓ Stimulation and sustaining of intrinsic motivation (Engel, 2015, p. 108; Ostoff, 2016, p. 3)

✓ Improvement of observational skills and memory (Ostoff, 2012, 2016)

✓ Deepening of learning (Engel, 2015, p. 48; Fullan, Quinn, & McEachen, 2018; Ostoff, 2016, p. 5)

✓ Increased academic outcomes (Engel, 2015, p. 174; Goodwin, 2018, p. ix)

✓ Enhancement of cognitive skills (Barell, 2003, p. 5; Ostoff, 2016, p. 12)

Fullan and colleagues (2018) identify creativity and curiosity as one of the six global competencies required for deep learning in today's world. They associate "asking the right inquiry questions" and "considering and pursuing novel ideas and solutions" with this competency. They point to the thinking of Daan Roosegaarde, a Dutch designer, architect, and innovator, to exemplify this competency in action. Roosegarde, a self-proclaimed reformer, asserts that when pondering how to make the world a better place, he always begins with *"why are things as they are?"* As an example, this innovator shared his wondering about why we spend so much money on cars only to drive them on roads that conform to Middle Age design principles. This question led him to develop paints that charge with solar energy by day and emit light at night (Fullan et al., p. 13). This innovative designer generated suggestions for learning environments to support student wondering and imagining, beginning with: "Create learning driven by curiosity where 'learners are infiltrators and shapers of the future.' This means working on issues of relevance to themselves and the world" (p. 14).

Harvard researcher Susan Engel (2015) distinguishes between two types of curiosity identified in the classrooms she studied: curiosity that emerges in the context of classroom activities and the type of curiosity that "erupt[s] around the margins of the classroom" (p. 89). The former type can be planned and structured by teachers, as did Mrs. Barkley for her biology students. Curiosity occurring on "the margins" typically grows out of interactions resulting in out-of-the-box wonderings. Too often we dismiss these questions, fearing they may take us too far afield from our pacing guides. While the primary emphasis in this chapter is on structuring classroom activities that invite exploratory questions related to academic goals, we will also consider the conditions that nurture the spontaneous type of curiosity and address how we can balance the two.

NURTURING CURIOSITY—DEVELOPING STUDENT CAPACITY TO ASK EXPLORATORY QUESTIONS

> Children are naturally curious, but their school experience appears to dampen that curiosity and produce students who are not.

Children are naturally curious, but their school experience appears to dampen that curiosity and produce students who are not. Meanwhile, many children remain curious outside of the schoolhouse. This calls to question the very nature of curiosity.

Goodwin (2020) differentiates between *state* curiosity, which is temporary and task specific, and *trait* curiosity, a deeper, more internalized type. This distinction is not unlike that identified by Canadian psychologist Daniel Berlyne, whose groundbreaking research contrasted *perceptual* to *epistemic* curiosity. Perceptual curiosity results from novel, puzzling, or ambiguous stimuli and, like state curiosity, is time or situation bound. (*Think miracle berries.*) Berlyne viewed epistemic curiosity as an individual attribute that drives individuals to push the boundaries of knowledge (Livio, 2017, pp. 4–5). Engel (2015) noted that questions growing out of epistemic curiosity go beyond who, what, when, and where to focus on why and how (p. 28). (*Think Roosegaarde's solar-energy paint.*)

Exploratory questions, as defined here, can spring from any type of curiosity. Our interest is in developing both the skill and the will that result in students forming and expressing these questions. Because curiosity in all forms is in short supply among today's students, the development of the capacity to ask exploratory questions must be viewed as a two-step process: (1) activating and unleashing curiosity and (2) developing student skills in conveying the curiosity through a well-formed question. Focusing on students' ways of thinking about curiosity and questions is a springboard for this process.

> **Begin With the Mindframe.** *I use questions to channel my curiosity and spark my creativity.*

This mindframe is an affirmation of the belief that all students are curious and creative and that we, as teachers, are interested in their wonderings. Further, it is an invitation to each student to share these with members of their classroom community. Most importantly, the mindframe is a call for students to reflect on their current beliefs and behaviors related to exploratory questions.

As students advance through school, routines and procedures define their role as that of responder to teacher questions and instructions, not initiator of their own wonderings or inquiries. This lived experience in school contributes to beliefs and attitudes that govern thoughts and behaviors. This is particularly true for compliant students who seek to please their teachers by abiding by these traditional classroom norms. When curiosity tugs at their attention, they may tell themselves, as I did when a student: *Hold your questions of curiosity to ask at home or to pose after class to a teacher who might be interested. Don't allow your wonderings to lead you too far afield from the focus the teacher has established for a lesson. Learn what's expected so you can give the teacher what he wants at test time.* While there are students who have the courage to express their curiosities and certainly teachers who welcome these expressions, far too many students have learned how to play by these implicit rules.

A first step in reversing student attitudes and beliefs is to challenge them, to communicate that we value their curiosity and welcome the questions that express them. Afford time and opportunities for students to make meaning of this mindframe and engage in dialogue about its value. Consider introducing the mindframe with a prompt or prop. Among many possibilities are the following:

- Display photos of inventors or explorers—for example, Leonardo, Thomas Edison, Marie Curie, George Washington Carver, Picasso, Caroline Herschel, Einstein, and Patricia Bath. Ask what these individuals had in common. Follow up by having small, collaborative groups generate the questions that may have driven these innovators and circumstances that may have led to their questions.

- Introduce a novel object to the classroom. Remember the moustaches that Mrs. Ray hung from the ceiling of her third-grade classroom to build her students' curiosity about asking questions?

- Ask students to generate a list of the top three things about which they are curious in one of their areas of interest—for example, sports, fashion, music, art, and so forth. Inquire as to whether they've expressed these curiosities to others or attempted to find out more about them. Then ask them to speculate about what piques their curiosity.

Whatever strategy you choose to surface students' thinking about curiosity, conclude by inviting them to share what might support their curiosity in the classroom and what gets in the way.

As with other mindframes, post this one publicly as a daily reminder to you and your students to ask the why, how, what if, and imagine questions and to use these to keep the excitement and passion for learning alive.

TEACH SKILLS AND STRATEGIES

Most would agree that curiosity is more a disposition than a skill. Why then offer a set of skills and strategies to support this category of questions? Students need tools to support thinking and verbalization of that thinking. Some students have greater need of such tools than others.

As is true in fostering other categories of student questions, sample prompts and stems provide both a tool and a reminder to every child that we expect them to form questions of their own. Figure 5.1 provides a beginner set that can serve to cue and scaffold student forming and framing of exploratory questions.

Identifying skills and suggesting opportunities for use can reinforce expectations associated with exploratory questions. The sample prompts and stems serve to scaffold skill development. Provide students with a copy of this chart for easy reference and afford them periodic opportunities to reflect and self-assess their progress in developing the identified skills.

MODEL QUESTION-ASKING THROUGH THINK-ALOUDS

John Barell, an early advocate of cultivating and capitalizing on student curiosity in the classroom, is a strong proponent of teacher modeling of curiosity during the act of teaching. He offers this list of stems for use in a routine and authentic manner:

- What I am curious about is . . .
- What I do not yet understand is . . .
- I really want to find out . . .

FIGURE 5.1 Skills and Sample Prompts Associated With Exploratory Questions

SKILL	USE WHEN	SAMPLE PROMPTS AND STEMS
Express curiosity.	• You are perplexed. • You have a genuine wondering.	• I wonder why _____. • How might we _____? • Have you ever thought about _____?
Challenge a traditional way of thinking about a topic.	• You wonder if there might be a different way of approaching a topic or solving a problem. • You wonder why a particular way of thinking about a topic seems to dominate thinking.	• What might be an alternative way of thinking? • What if _____? • What's another way of thinking of _____? • Can we imagine another way to approach this?
Test new ideas.	• You have a different way of thinking and want to know how others react.	• I am thinking _____. What do you think? • Imagine _____. How might this play out? • What if we set aside what we've always assumed?

- The mysteries and puzzles that really intrigue me are . . .

- If I could be somebody else . . . or visit another time period, this is what I'd want to discover . . .

- I really wonder why . . .

- What intrigues me is . . . (pp. 49–50)

Barell suggests offering these same stems to students as prompts for reflection and writing in their journals.

Teachers of young students consistently report that one of their initial challenges is to teach students what a question looks and sounds like. While not denying the curiosity of children in the early grades, they note that many of these young learners don't know the difference between a statement and a question and that explicit instruction and consistent modeling are required. This was the case with the first graders in Kehaulani Bohannon's class featured in the following lesson.

> "If we wish to foster curiosity, wonder and skepticism, there are questions we can ask ourselves often enough that they can become mental habits for ourselves and for our students."—John Barell, 2003, p. 49.

Classroom Questioners at Work

Kehaulani Bohannon designed a multistep lesson to engage her first graders in meeting their daily learning target: *I can ask and answer questions when I investigate animal ears*. The purpose was for students to use what they had been learning about vibrations and sounds as they began their investigation of animal ears. Throughout the lesson, Mrs. Bohannon asked questions and thought aloud as she shared her wonderings with her students. As she carefully orchestrated a lesson designed to culminate in students developing and sharing exploratory questions, she used her own carefully planned questions to engage and model for the students.

The primary text for the lesson was *What If You Had Animal Ears?* by Sandra Markle. Mrs. Bohannon donned a pair of elephant ears as she began reading this nonfiction account of five different animals' ears. As she read about elephant ears, the first feature in the book, she stopped to identify noticings that led her to her wondering: *Could these ears get in the way of an elephant?* She continued reading, stopping to think aloud with students about the ears of four other animals.

Following the reading, she organized students into four collaborative groups to focus on the ears of one of the other animals featured in the text. Their assignment was to share noticings and then to generate wonderings in preparation for their reporters' sharing with the whole group. As Mrs. Bohannon circulated to listen to small group dialogue, she continued to ask the students questions and to think-aloud with them as appropriate. Video 5.2, "Collaborative Generation of Exploratory Questions," highlights this teacher's modeling and the emerging student questions. ■

Most elementary teachers rely heavily on think-alouds to model expected cognitive processing and outcomes. While used less frequently as students move into upper grades, it is no less effective. As previously suggested, thinking aloud about questions of curiosity is a particularly powerful strategy. Not only do teacher expressions of curiosity model related question stems, they also reinforce the fun and adventure associated with just wondering.

ADOPT ROUTINES AND PROTOCOLS

Thinking Routines. A number of thinking routines are particularly appropriate to the nurturing of exploratory questions because they invite student wondering via open-ended prompts. Among the more widely used are See-Think-Wonder, Think-Puzzle-Explore, and Claim, Support, Question. Two books by Ritchhart and colleagues, *Making Thinking Visible* (Ritchhart, Church, & Morrison, 2011) and *The Power of Making Thinking Visible* (Ritchhart & Church, 2020), serve as handy resources for individual and team planning.

Ritchhart (2015) writes that "a routine is more than an activity." Designed for repeated use over time, a thinking routine comes to function as a "pattern of behavior for both individuals and the group," becoming embedded in the class culture (p. 170). While activities are episodic and related to a particular learning outcome, thinking routines are intended to become mental frames, enduring structures that can be activated by students within and outside of school. When attempting to nourish wonder and curiosity as mental frames for our students, thinking routines are a go-to resource.

Protocols. These structures define step-by-step procedures to lead individuals and groups to the attainment of a desired goal, including creation of questions of curiosity. Engel (2015) reports that such approaches pique curiosity and enhance motivation (p. 90). Others have found students do not tend to embrace questions given to them by others, that a question becomes genuine for the students only when they ask it themselves—that is, when they see a contradiction or puzzle they did not see before and set out to explain it" (Cifone, as cited by Ostroff, 2016, p. 49).

The Questioning Circle, which follows, is a protocol appropriate for use with upper elementary through high school students. This protocol affords students an opportunity to provide feedback on individually crafted questions and to reach consensus around a question to investigate collaboratively.

Questioning Circle

The Questioning Circle is a text-based protocol that can be used to stimulate student curiosity and identify a question for further investigation. As with all text protocols, students prepare by individually reading and reflecting on a teacher-selected passage to identify a segment of the text that raises a question about which they are truly curious, a question that goes beyond the facts into the why or how of the issue. Students refer to sample prompts and stems as needed to formulate a question of interest. They mark the place in the text from which their question emerges and carefully word the question to ensure clarity and understandability.

The teacher assigns students to small groups of three for sharing, dialogue, and collaborative investigation. Students follow these steps as they listen to one another's questions and select one for group dialogue.

(Continued)

(Continued)

- Each group designates a facilitator and a time-keeper to manage group functioning.

- One group member volunteers to go first and proceeds to point others to the place in the text that stimulated her question. She reads the passage and then shares her question. She does not elaborate or begin responding to her question. While she speaks, others listen actively. (up to one minute)

- Following the offering of the text and question, all group members take time to think and jot down what the question says to them and whether and why the question is of personal interest. (one minute)

- After a minute or so of silence, the individual to the left of the speaker offers his quick reaction to the question, indicating what it means to him and expressing the extent to which the question piques his curiosity. (up to one minute)

- Talk proceeds in a clock-wise fashion, with other group members sharing their impressions. (no more than one minute per speaker)

- The author of the question summarizes what she heard and makes a final case for the importance of the question. This ends Round 1. (up to two minutes)

- The group engages in two additional rounds, to surface the questions of all members.

- The group facilitator leads discussion to select one of the three questions for investigation and dialogue. The group may modify the selected question or write a new question that draws from the group's collective thinking. (up to ten minutes)

- Following question selection, group dialogue affords members the opportunity to surface their initial thinking and generate ideas for further investigation of the question. (up to five minutes)

- The teacher provides a half-sheet of paper to each small group for scribing their question.

- Teams present their questions, looking for patterns across all questions.

- Following class, the teacher creates a schedule for investigations and plans how to support each group's investigation. ∎

Affording a safe environment for peer interaction usually serves to enhance an individual's initial thinking and wondering. Thinking routines and protocols provide a certain safety net for students by providing structure, clarifying expectations, and minimizing uncertainty. By helping to level the playing field, they increase the likelihood that all students will be more likely to assume the risk of asking more out-of-the-box questions.

Classroom Questioners at Work

Stephanie Hendrix designed a protocol to use at the beginning of a unit on World War II for the purpose of surfacing her sixth graders' interests and questions. She began by selecting and assembling artifacts and readings associated with identified themes of the war to display at five stations. She carefully created collaborative teams to rotate through the stations over the course of two class periods. Mrs. Hendrix designed a step-by-step process, with accompanying tools, that led students to identify issues about which they were curious and formulate questions to express the wonderings. Students subsequently assessed, prioritized, and adopted questions to guide their inquiries throughout the unit. Video 5.3, "Activating Sixth Graders' Curiosity About Historical Issues," illustrates how this process came alive for these students. ∎

Like Mrs. Hendrix, many teachers are developing and adapting class protocols that fit their community contexts, their students, and their subject area. For example, teacher/author Trevor MacKenzie leads his students on periodic *curiosity walks*, going outside to collect items from nature that stir interest and curiosity. Students store their treasures in a knapsack or bag after close observations during which they may use a magnifying glass, render a sketch, and/or jot down their observations in a small journal. Upon return to the classroom, they participate in a *sharing circle* to describe their discoveries and questions (*Inquiry Mindset*, 2018,

"If students are to ask deep questions about complex academic content, they need time and structures to develop and express their wonderings. Additionally, questioners require a setting and a set of supportive procedures for engagement of others in the investigative process."—Wendy Ostroff, 2016, p. 17

p. 75). MacKenzie also maintains a wonder wall personalized with the names, photos, and accompanying thought bubbles for each student. Students routinely record their wonderings, and the teacher acknowledges and addresses the wonderings at appropriate points in a unit.

INCORPORATE INTO DAILY LESSONS

Daily routine can be the enemy of the blossoming of curiosity in classrooms. Susan Engel (2015), an eminent scholar on childhood curiosity, identifies two primary barriers to nurturing and advancing expressions of curiosity: the "plans and scripts" that regulate what transpires daily in most classrooms, and the "pressure to get a lot of things 'done' each day" (p. 103). The dominant script in most classrooms continues to be the Initiate-Respond-Evaluate (IRE) model, wherein teachers *initiate* almost all classroom questions, designate volunteers to *respond*, and *evaluate* their responses (Mehan, 1979). This script is characterized by teacher control and limited student talk. When teachers commit to release responsibility to students, they interrupt the patterns established by IRE. The role and responsibilities associated with teachers as activators of student questions, outlined in Chapter 2, nurture curiosity as well as student questions.

> Daily routine can be the enemy of the blossoming of curiosity in classrooms.

Teacher planning is key if opportunities for student expression of exploratory questions are to become integrated into the fabric of student learning. A number of considerations guide effective planning:

- Ensure that students have sufficient knowledge to form an exploratory question but not so much as to squelch the thirst for additional knowing. Those who have studied curiosity and exploratory questioning emphasize that a certain amount of surface knowledge is required to spark curiosity and stimulate questions (e.g., Engel, 2015; Leslie, 2004; Ostroff, 2012). For example, Leslie writes that curiosity does not emerge "in the abstract" but "depends on factual information" (p. 122). On the other hand, he notes that too many facts "kill curiosity" (p. 115). Finding the sweet spot is an art; it is not reducible to a formula. Remember that curiosity oftentimes emerges when students identify a gap between the known and the unknown and sense that they have the ability to fill the gap. Design lessons and units that build in these potentially productive gaps.

- Identify strategic points in a lesson to incorporate formal structures for activating curiosity and attendant questions. Exploratory questions can be elicited early in a unit of study to enable student choice and self-direction as students move from surface to deep knowledge. On the other hand, some teachers integrate opportunities for students to form exploratory questions to move from deep to transfer learning. Determination of the most appropriate stage in a learning cycle depends upon the nature of the big ideas associated with a unit.

- Integrate ongoing opportunities for students to express and record unprompted wonderings and questions borne of curiosity. Beyond the use of designed experiences and formal structures for generation and pursuit of exploratory questions, the daily rhythms of classes can provide opportunities for students to record spontaneous wonderings. For example, when Think Time 2 is fully integrated into the patterns of class interaction, students have a moment to process, wonder, and express wondering. When there are occasional one- to two-minute pauses for reflection, students can identify knowledge gaps and think beyond the "givens" to create exploratory questions.

> Beyond the use of designed experiences and formal structures for generation and pursuit of exploratory questions, the daily rhythms of classes can provide opportunities for students to record spontaneous wonderings.

Student expressions of curiosity will not occur in a "business as usual" classroom. Teacher commitment and intentionality are essential.

MAKE TIME AND SPACE

Two frequently used strategies for eliciting student exploratory questions are (1) timeouts for student reflection and recording in their journals and (2) invitations to students to post their wonderings on a reflection or curiosity wall. Note the need for a few minutes of downtime to allow for reflection and writing. Many teachers with whom I have worked invite students to affix the prompts and stems for exploratory questions inside their journals. These can inspire exploratory thinking for all students.

All students deserve the opportunity, and "for our most at-risk students, time to wonder and wander is essential" (Ostroff, 2016, p. 7). Too often the curiosity of low-achieving, at-risk students is blunted by rote learning, endless worksheets, and low expectations. These students have the most to gain from strategies than ignite questions and inspire excitement.

Not only do students require time to form their questions, they also need built-in time to pursue answers through tapping into reliable sources (Engel, 2015, p. 191). When creating weekly schedules that incorporate time for differentiation and self-guided learning, time must be allocated for students to explore, individually and collaboratively, the learning seeded by their questions.

> Too often the curiosity of low-achieving, at-risk students is blunted by rote learning, endless worksheets, and low expectations. These students have the most to gain from strategies than ignite questions and inspire excitement.

AFFORD PRACTICE WITH FEEDBACK

Self-assessment is the best form of feedback, particularly when focusing on questions strongly associated with a disposition. While teachers can design experiences to activate student curiosity and scaffold resulting question formulation, only students can gauge the extent to which the resulting questions are expressions of authentic curiosity. Only students know whether the curiosity is a temporary phenomenon (state curiosity) or leads to a deeper, more-lasting question that will motivate them over time.

As you design experiences to incite curiosity and launch student research, consider integrating thinking routines or protocols into the lesson. Provide students with opportunities to self-assess their questions by using Criteria for Exploratory Questions (Figure 5.2). Invite them to individually and silently examine a selected question. Ask students to jot down a rationale for their assessments—*Why did I rate as I did? What's behind my thinking?*

FIGURE 5.2   Criteria for Exploratory Questions

✓ *Motivates me to want to find out more about this area.* Focuses on something I care enough about to become excited as I research.

✓ *Has the potential to make a difference.* Discovering more about this might make a difference in my life and/or in the lives of others.

✓ *Is clearly and precisely stated.* Suggests where I might begin research to learn more about the topic.

✓ *Is understandable.* Clearly communicates to others.

Self-assessment can be augmented by peer assessment. When students have an opportunity to think out loud with a partner, they benefit from both hearing themselves and hearing the feedback they may receive from a partner. Following individual self-assessment, pair students with thought partners for sharing their questions and ratings. Culminate this activity by facilitating a brief whole-class dialogue focused on these questions: *What are we learning about our capacity to ask exploratory questions? In what ways are these questions valuable to our learning?*

> Nondirective feedback, consisting primarily of questions to continue student thinking about the dimensions of their curiosity, can be effective.

What about teacher feedback on the quality of student exploratory questions? Because of the dynamic and fluid nature of these questions, less is more. Nondirective feedback, consisting primarily of questions to continue student thinking about the dimensions of their curiosity, can be effective. More important, however, is genuine, positive feedback that communicates to students our excitement about their learning. This can be verbal, but the nonverbals—the smiles and other facial expressions and gestures signaling our own enthusiasm—are often the most significant.

INVITE STUDENT REFLECTION

Curiosity thrives in classrooms where student wonderings are routinely acknowledged and celebrated. Celebrations are more authentic when connected to success in meeting individual and collective goals. Among the strategies a teacher might adopt to facilitate student goal setting and reflection in this important area are the following:

- Periodically, every three to four weeks, plan a mini-session to refocus student attention on the mindframes for their questioning. Ask each student to think about the extent to which they believe they have been consciously focusing on one or more of these. Have them select the one they feel they've been using most consistently and effectively and move to a designated place in the room to join others who made the same choice. Provide three minutes or so for students to share evidence of their progress with those around them. Facilitate a quick sharing-out to acknowledge progress.

- Invite students to bring one object to class that represents something about which they are curious. Perhaps they wonder how or why it works as it does or where it came from. Ask them what about the object drew their attention and sparked their curiosity. When giving the assignment, the teacher might model. Pair students with a partner and instruct them to share their objects with one another. After pair sharing, ask pairs to talk about how it feels to be curious and how often they have that feeling when they are engaged in learning in school. Engage in whole class dialogue in response to this question: *How might we support one another in creating a classroom where curiosity thrives?*

"Joyous Exploration"

A significant research base in the field of psychology focuses on curiosity. Multiple researchers have designed research-based inventories to assess an individual's propensity toward this trait. One such inventory consists of five dimensions, one of which is named *joyous exploration*. This four-item scale seems particularly appropriate for use in the classroom. Consider creating a rating scale for your students using these items.

1. I view challenging situations as an opportunity to grow and learn.

2. I seek out situations where it is likely that I will have to think in depth about something.

3. I enjoy learning about subjects that are unfamiliar to me.

4. I find it fascinating to learn information. ■

In Closing: *Changing the Equation*

Tapping into student curiosity and surfacing their questions offer the single greatest opportunities for empowering our learners. Through this process, we can transform roles, responsibilities, and relationships in our classrooms. This can transfer the locus of control from teacher to students as students assume increased responsibility for helping to chart the direction of their learning and set learning goals they care about. Additionally, when teachers invite and honor student questions, we communicate to students that we value their thinking and care about the emotions they bring to our learning community.

Researcher Susan Engel writes "We've had experimental evidence for at least the past fifty years to support the idea that children's intrinsic interest is the most powerful ingredient for learning" (2015, p. 108). Few of us would disagree. Engel and others who have studied curiosity in the classroom link curiosity to intrinsic motivation. This is the strongest argument for partnering with our students to ensure that curiosity is alive and well within individuals and the classroom and broader school community.

Spotlight: Online Opportunities for Exploratory Questions

Begin with the end in mind. When the goal is stimulation and expression of student curiosity through exploratory questions, the challenge is to find catalysts that students can access online. Possibilities include visual or auditory displays (e.g., videos, podcasts, artworks, or cartoons) and offline observations. When students are learning from home, they have a real-life environment, inside and outside, to investigate and wonder about. As we seek to uncork curiosity from afar, we begin by thinking outside of the box ourselves.

Highlight the appropriate mindframe, skills, and tools for students in the lesson where particular question types will be emphasized. The mindframe we are nurturing within our students is, *I use questions to channel my curiosity and spark my creativity.* On days when you seek to engage this very emotional side of student learning, the mindframe might serve as a masthead on the day's landing page. The skills and sample prompts, Figure 5.1, and Criteria for Exploratory Questions, Figure 5.2, need to be called out to students on these days.

Strategically position formal requests for exploratory questions in the unit or lesson. The hope is that this type of question will emerge spontaneously as students engage in learning a new topic. Because distance learning is not highly facilitative of spontaneous expressions, deciding upon a potentially fruitful point in the lesson to prompt is critical. The beginning and end of units are the two most strategic positions for intentional and active solicitation. However, as suggested below, establishing an online space where students can post their wonderings whenever they occur is also recommended.

Adapt protocols and response routines for online use. See-Think-Wonder is my favorite thinking routine for scaffolding exploratory questions at all grade levels. I have used this to evoke student questions following the viewing of a video, the study of a painting, the review of a document, and for other print and visual stimuli. The see and think portions focus attention and bring forward prior experience leading to authentic wonders. The wonders can be captured via Padlet, Jamboard, Flipgrid, SeeSaw or other apps with which students are familiar.

The Questioning Circle can be used by having students bring questions created while engaged in self-paced reading to their community learning in a synchronous environment. Older learners can work in multiple breakout rooms via Zoom, Microsoft Teams, or another meeting platform where three students follow the protocol as they would if in a classroom. Each group then selects a question to bring forward to the whole group for sharing and planning of an investigation. Younger

(Continued)

(Continued)

students might report their questions via Padlet or Jamboard, in the whole community setting or offline through SeeSaw or Flipgrid.

Carefully select a limited number of tech tools (i.e., platforms and apps) for use by a class of students. Adam Clark features student creative endeavors via podcasts supported by Anchor.fm. For example, students create questions of curiosity and engage in research using reliable resources and share these through podcasts. In lieu of a podcast, students could create videos to share with others using Screencastify or a slide presentation via Pear Deck.

Tracy Ray prompts students to wonder about what they would like to ask an identified expert when they are learning remotely. For example, in Spring 2020, her students prepared questions for a local weatherman who answered them virtually while they were learning remotely. She has connected students with experts around the world using Zoom.

When learning remotely, students can be encouraged to share their wonderings on a virtual Wonder Wall. This can be created in any LMS. Student wonders can be appropriately incorporated into community meetings supported by a selected meeting platform. ∎

Curtain Call: Revisiting Key Ideas Related to Exploratory Questions

KEY IDEAS	QUESTIONS FOR PERSONAL REFLECTION
1. Exploratory questions are questions that result from student wondering, from deep curiosity.	• What are you doing to nurture and surface these kinds of questions in your classroom and school? • How often do student questions lead students to investigate and explore issues related to academic content?
2. Exploratory questions, those emerging from student curiosity, yield benefits for student learning.	• What examples can you offer of student curiosity leading to increased motivation and performance? • Why do you think student questions emerging from curiosity lead to increased interest and performance?
3. Exploratory questions can emerge from multiple types of curiosity—perceptual and epistemic, or state and trait.	• Which type of curiosity do you most often notice in your students? To what do you attribute this? • What ideas do you have for advancing both of these types of curiosity?
4. To increase exploratory questions, teachers focus on activating curiosity and developing student skills as questioners.	• What strategies are you using to stimulate curiosity among *all* students? • How can we best develop student skills and will to ask exploratory questions?
5. Mindframe: *I use questions to channel my curiosity and spark my creativity.*	• To what extent do your students believe teachers value curiosity and the questions that result? • How might you go about facilitating changes in student beliefs about the role of curiosity in their learning?
6. Sample prompts and stems can both scaffold the writing of questions and cue students to express curiosity.	• What experience, if any, have you had in teaching students to use sample prompts? To what extent did students use these? • What other prompts and stems (beyond those provided in Figure 5.1) might you use with your students?
7. Teacher modeling of curiosity is perhaps the most important way to encourage student curiosity and questions.	• In what ways are you currently modeling curiosity to your students and your colleagues? • What are some other techniques you might employ to demonstrate curiosity and excitement as you teach?

(Continued)

(Continued)

KEY IDEAS	QUESTIONS FOR PERSONAL REFLECTION
8. Thinking routines provide a mental map leading to the activation of curiosity.	• Why do you believe that routine use of these types of routines might support long-term curiosity? • Examine the thinking routines on the Project Zero website (http://pz.harvard .edu/thinking-routines) that seem appropriate to your students. Select one to try out.
9. Design learning experiences that tap into student curiosity.	• At what point(s) might formal activation of curiosity and exploratory questions fit into one of your upcoming units of study? What purposes might such an experience serve? • Consider the strategies featured in the three videos in this chapter (i.e., biology, first-grade, and sixth-grade classes.) Which of these might be adaptable to your classroom and students?
10. Providing periodic opportunities for self-assessment and reflection are important.	• Which of the strategies mentioned in these two sections of the chapter might you being willing to try out with your students? • How often do you provide time-outs for student reflection?

CHAPTER 6

Dialogic Questions

Clarifying and Deepening Understanding

> I use questions to understand other perspectives and to engage in collaborative thinking and learning.

STUDENT MINDFRAME

The purpose of dialogic questions is to get to the root of why "a thing is so or might be so," whether the intent is to more deeply understand academic content or another's perspective. Dialogic questions are the tools students can use to dig deeper to extend their personal understandings while collaboratively pursuing new insights. Two categories of benefits result from student engagement in purposeful dialogue: increased academic achievement *and* preparation for participation in democratic life (e.g., Alexander, 2020; Juzwik et al., 2013; McCann, 2014; Nystrand, 1997). Hattie found dialogue to have an effect size of $d = 0.82$, translating into over two years of growth for a year in school (Hattie, 2012, p. 72).

"Children construct meaning not only from the interaction between what they newly encounter and what they already know, but also from verbal interaction with others—parents, teachers, and peers—and the worlds those others inhabit. . . . In turn, this interaction is critical not just for children's understanding of the kind of knowledge with which schools deal but also for the development of their very identity, their sense of self and worth."
(Alexander, 2020, p. 13)

Dialogue, as defined here, is more than a simple volleying back and forth of talk between the teacher and students. Dialogue engages students in speaking, listening to, and questioning one another and can lead to a synthesis of ideas, where the whole is greater than the sum of the individual parts. It can also contribute to increased respect for others and their ideas.

Alexander (2020) argues that dialogic exchanges are *collective, supportive, reciprocal, deliberative, cumulative*, and *purposeful* (p. 131). These features are shaped by the questions that drive dialogue. Dialogic questions enable *reciprocal* thinking, a give-and-take that supports *collective* reasoning and leads to a *cumulative* outcome. Further, these questions support *deliberative* thinking and speaking that are *purposeful* in nature, not rambling or undisciplined. Finally, the best dialogic questions are *supportive* in that they are worded in a nonthreatening manner. Through the asking and answering of questions in a dialogic exchange, students assist one another in reaching deeper, better informed interpretations or conclusions.

BROADENING PERSPECTIVES—DEVELOPING STUDENT CAPACITY TO ASK DIALOGIC QUESTIONS

Dialogic exchanges are not the dominant pattern of classroom talk in most of today's classrooms. As a result, students receive neither the coaching nor the practice to support the development of dispositions and skills essential to this more complex and sophisticated form of interaction.

> **Begin With the Mindframe.** *I ask questions to understand other perspectives and to engage in collaborative thinking and learning.*

Dillon (1994) claims that an important disposition for dialogue is "a *basic willingness to talk things over with other people* . . . explore the matter with them, hear other views, and come up with a good answer to our question, one that satisfies us in some respect" (p. 45.) The mindframe underpinning dialogic questions inspires students to question when someone voices an interpretation or perspective that does not match their own or when they wish to learn more about a perspective. This invites joint exploration of a topic or issue by asking others to surface views that the questioner can consider and use to test, modify, expand, or even affirm, his own answer.

Students need to understand that dialogic questions are about *both* identifying what is behind another's thinking—whether it first appears to be right or wrong, good or bad—*and* prompting others to contribute to the collective pool of knowledge and perspectives so as to create a richer, more complete understanding of a particular topic or issue. The former demonstrates respect for diverse points of view, while the latter enables collaborative thinking and learning. These two functions of dialogic questions are important within and beyond the walls of classrooms.

> Students need to understand that dialogic questions are about *both* identifying what is behind another's thinking—whether it first appears to be right or wrong, good or bad—*and* prompting others to contribute to the collective pool of knowledge and perspectives so as to create a richer, more complete understanding of a particular topic or issue.

Because of the multiple layers of meaning embedded in this mindframe, unpacking and examining the wording with students is critically important. The mindframe, once again, embodies the why—why it is important to learn how to form this type of question and to exercise the courage required to ask, not as a challenge to others but as a request to share thinking aloud to build greater understanding. Setting aside time for students to relate this mindframe to their everyday lives can assist them in appreciating its value in the classroom.

TEACH SKILLS AND STRATEGIES

Dialogic questions are perhaps the most challenging for students to frame and ask. In part, this is because they have so few examples of adults modeling this type of questioning. Hattie (2012) reports the dominance of monologue over dialogue in classrooms. Not only do most students lack classroom experience, they have few, if any, examples of dialogue outside of school. A decreasing number of families congregate at the dinner table for the kind of meal-time conversations many of us remember from our youth. And cable television features talk-show hosts who ask questions to have others echo their own points of view rather than seeking to surface and explore different perspectives. The absence of modeling results in students neither understanding when dialogic questions might be appropriate nor what these kinds of questions sound like.

Skills and Stems to Scaffold. The "Use When" column of Figure 6.1 specifies when the formation of such a question is appropriate. The "Sample Prompts and Stems" offers beginning tools students can use as they convert wonderings or doubts into words. While this chart is not exhaustive, it does provide a foundational resource for students. Simply placing this in student hands is not sufficient. Consider designing a mini-lesson that helps students unpack each skill and related scaffolds. Encourage students to skim this chart on a regular basis, particularly prior to an extended dialogue that is an integral part of a daily lesson.

Listening Is Prerequisite. Another skill set that is essential to dialogic questioning is listening. Students must listen with intentionality and deliberate thought if they are to engage in dialogic questioning. It is important to teach students the difference between listening and hearing. In our book, *Questioning for Classroom Discussion*, Beth Sattes and I suggest that teachers assist students in using these specific behaviors as they listen:

- Use silence after a classmate stops speaking to think about what was said and to compare the speaker's thinking to one's own (Think Time 2).

- Pause before adding one's own comment or posing a question to ensure that the speaker has completed her thinking (Think Time 2).

- Ask questions to better understand a speaker's point of view.

- Accurately paraphrase what another says.

- Look at the speaker and give nonverbal cues that you are paying attention. (Walsh & Sattes, 2015, p. 40)

FIGURE 6.1 Sample Prompt and Stems for Dialogic Questions

SKILL	USE WHEN	SAMPLE PROMPTS AND STEMS
Pose questions to get behind the thinking of a speaker.	• You wonder how someone arrived at a certain answer or conclusion. • You'd like to know what evidence or data the speaker is using to support his/her idea. • You're wondering about the steps or logic used by the speaker.	• I hadn't thought of it that way. What led you to this conclusion? • Would this always be true? Can you think of something that might change your way of thinking? • What makes you say that? • What evidence supports this way of thinking?
Ask questions to identify a speaker's assumptions (or beliefs).	• You wonder if the speaker's personal biases are causing him to overlook factual evidence. • You are curious as to why someone holds a particular point of view.	• What makes you say that? • What experiences have you had related to _____? • I'd like to get behind your thinking about _____.
Ask questions to surface and examine one's own assumptions.	• You are preparing to explain or defend your perspective or conclusion. • You are encountering a different way of thinking—one that at first seems counter to your beliefs.	• How are my personal beliefs affecting my openness to others? • What has contributed to my position on this issue? • Am I open to listening to this argument even though it is counter to my beliefs?
Ask questions that challenge "group-think."	• Members of a group seem to be blindly accepting all statements and comments. • You sense that members of a group are not comfortable challenging others' ideas.	• What's another way of thinking about _____? • I wonder if we can think "out of the box" about this. • What if we came at this issue from another direction? • Imagine _____. How might this affect our thinking?
Encourages nonparticipants to speak.	• You notice that a few individuals are dominating a discussion. • You observe that someone is not participating in class dialogue.	• What do others think about _____? • I'm curious as to what someone who hasn't yet spoken thinks about this.

Use of the pauses, particularly Think Time 2, during a conversation provides students and teachers with the opportunity to make meaning of the statement and formulate follow-up dialogic questions.

Three Purposes of Dialogic Questions. Alexander (2020) identifies three broad purposes of dialogue—initiate, probe, and expand—that serve as useful categories for dialogic questions. Figure 6.2 draws from his elaboration of these three (p. 148). These three purposes assume that dialogue is cumulative, that the back-and-forth talk extends thinking by moving through progressive stages. This can be a helpful frame to orient students to the purposes of dialogic questions.

FIGURE 6.2 Three Categories of Dialogic Questions

1. INITIATE	
PURPOSE	**SAMPLE PROMPT OR STEM**
Elicit observation or opinion	What do you think about _____?
Invite reflection or speculation	What would happen if _____?
	Why do you think that _____?

2. PROBE	
PURPOSE	**SAMPLE PROMPT OR STEM**
Probe or test the thinking behind a response.	Why do you say that _____?
	How do you know that _____?
	Will you explain _____?
Clarify the thinking behind a response or the way it has been expressed.	Do you mean [paraphrase speaker comment]?
	Can you put this another way?
Invite evaluation.	What do you think about _____?
	Is _____ correct? What's your evidence?

3. EXPAND	
PURPOSE	**SAMPLE PROMPT OR STEM**
Expand the initial exchange.	Can you give me another example of _____?
	Is there an alternative explanation of _____?
Sustain or develop a line of thinking through connected questions.	How does your response relate to a previous speaker's comment?
	I was thinking _____. In what ways might your comment relate to mine?

Student Questioners at Work

In this high school robotics lab, small groups of students engage in collaborative dialogue as they think together about designing robots and green cars for competition. One group focuses on redesign of their green car; another, on design of a robot. Team members question one another as they seek to design a winning entry. In this video clip, Video 6.2, "Dialogic Questions and Design Thinking," you'll listen in to these student-driven conversations. As these team members move their thinking forward, they incorporate the three broad purposes of dialogue—initiating, probing one another's ideas, and expanding and refining specs for the products they are designing. Krista Mintz and Britton Young, the instructors who guide these young designers' efforts, concur that question formation has improved the quality of student dialogue and ultimate design. ▪

Criteria for Crafting Dialogic Questions. Creating questions to initiate dialogue requires a higher level of skill than asking follow-up questions to probe or expand. The above sample stems and prompts are fairly standard or generic and can be used in conversations about a wide range of topics and issues. Questions to initiate dialogue, however, are more specific to the content area or issue under consideration and require a greater degree of conceptual thinking on the part of the student.

When forming a question to initiate dialogue, the questioner needs first to find an entry point to the topic that will generate divergent thinking; that is, she must identify a content focus for the question that is open to debate or deliberation. The questioner then faces the challenge of framing the question in a manner that provokes deep thinking. This relates to verb choice, the cognitive demand of the question. For example, action verbs—such as *imagine, speculate, analyze, predict*—are likely to engender deeper and more sustained thinking and responding than passive verbs. Additionally, the questioner is called upon to word the initiating question tactfully so as to invite everyone to respond without fear of embarrassment. These considerations can be presented to students as criteria for use in framing dialogic questions as shown in Figure 6.3.

FIGURE 6.3   Criteria for a Quality Dialogic Question

✓ *Focuses on an issue or topic for which there are multiple competing or conflicting points of view.*

✓ *Elicits reflection and speculation that lead to a personal opinion or a stance.*

✓ *Addresses a topic or issue that can generate deep and sustained thinking (more than a one- to two-word response).*

✓ *Uses open, nonjudgmental, invitational language that encourages everyone to take a position.*

✓ *Is understandable, stated in clear and precise terms.*

THINK-ALOUD AS YOU MODEL

Students lack good models for questions that initiate and sustain dialogue, and as a result, they have limited experience in classroom conversations that flow from such questions. Students do hear many questions day-in and day-out as they move through school; in fact, question-asking dominates a large portion of class time. Teachers ask on average about 100 questions per hour (Mohr, 1998) or one to three per minute (Gall, 1970). These questions help maintain teacher control and, as a result, minimize student speaking and participation.

Nystrand, a preeminent student of classroom discourse, conducted a large-scale study of 200 eighth- and ninth-grade English and social studies classrooms. He and his research team coded over 30,000 student and teacher questions from hundreds of classroom observations (Nystrand et al., 2003 p. 136). The data revealed three specific teacher questioning practices spurring students to ask questions: (1) the asking of authentic questions, (2) the use of uptake, and (3) high-level evaluation (p. 183). They define an *authentic question* as one for which the questioner has not predetermined an answer; *uptake* is when the teacher asks a student about a comment made by a previous student; and a *high level of evaluation* consists of an elaborated response, involving a follow-up question (pp. 145–146). These teacher questioning moves are noteworthy because of their high impact on student learning and because they can serve as models for students.

Questions that increase the length and depth of student speaking and create dialogical exchanges focus on quality over quantity. Teachers create these questions, which meet the following criteria, as a part of lesson design:

- Are "true" or authentic questions

- Are open ended and divergent—not convergent

- Stimulate responses at higher cognitive levels

- Engage students personally and emotionally (Walsh & Sattes, 2015, p. 17)

The beginning point in teaching students to form and ask dialogic questions is for teachers themselves to craft and pose such questions. For students to learn from teacher exemplars, they need to recognize the features of the question that make it effective for dialogue. When posing a question to initiate discussion, a teacher might write the question on the board and ask students to assess it using the criteria presented in Figure 6.3. By routinely focusing students on the characteristics of questions that open up dialogue, teachers are coaching their pupils to form better questions themselves.

Teacher modeling is the most powerful lever for enhancing student understanding of when and how to pose a dialogic question. Mercer and Dawes (2008) write

> If, in group discussions, pupils are expected to treat tentative ideas with respect, to ensure that different points of view are heard and to elaborate ideas so that everyone understands them, the teacher must do likewise when talking with the class. (p. 70)

To coach students in the what and why of these specific conversational moves, teachers are explicit about what they are doing and why. Following are examples of possible think-alouds teachers might use in each of the preceding situations.

Treating tentative ideas with respect	"Mark suggests that _____ is true. I do not yet have the evidence to support this claim, but I want to hear more. Mark, would you do some additional research to bring to us tomorrow?"
Ensuring that different points of view are heard	"Three of you have stated that you agree with Maya's interpretation of the main character's motives. I am intrigued by what you have said but would like to hear from someone with a different perspective. Who has another idea about what influenced the protagonist in our story? Hearing a different point of view will broaden my understanding of the author's character development."
Elaborating ideas so that everyone understands	"Jose told us _____. I am curious as to what is behind Jose's thinking so I'm going to ask him to say more. This will help me better understand how his thinking compares to mine."

When modeling and thinking aloud for students, it is helpful to use the language embedded in the tools provided to them. Referring to the skills featured in Figure 6.1 can reinforce the characteristics and requirements for dialogic questioning. Imagine that all members of a class were adopting the very same point of view in an argument. The teacher might ask a question to invite contrary opinions, saying, "I am wondering if we're engaging in a form of 'group-think' as we address this topic. Who can offer a view that represents a different way of thinking about this issue?"

Or consider the case of a teacher who wanted to encourage her students to ask questions to surface and examine their own assumptions when they seemed unable to hear their classmates who voiced points of view different from their own. She incorporated a personal anecdote into a think-aloud to illustrate her point.

"I know that sometimes it's difficult to listen carefully to those with whom we strongly disagree. I've experienced this challenge many times in conversations with friends. I remember vacationing with a cousin who is very into art. She wanted to visit a museum that featured modern art. I cringed and thought to myself, 'I find it a waste of time to look at so-called paintings that are meaningless.' I almost said this to my cousin, but then I asked myself: 'Why do you have this reaction to modern art?' 'What do you really know about it anyway?' As I responded to my own questions, I realized that I really didn't know enough to form an opinion, that I was making assumptions based on ignorance. So, I agreed to visit the museum with the understanding that my cousin would have patience with me and spend time helping me understand how this art spoke to her. As a result, I had a delightful dialogue with my cousin and began to understand why she felt as she did. I didn't completely change my view of modern art after the museum visit and dialogue, but I did have greater respect for my cousin's perspective. I hope that you will ask questions of one another when you have strong disagreements and that you'll answer one another non-defensively. It is very important that we learn to recognize when our assumptions prevent us from engaging in meaningful dialogue with another and then to ask questions that will increase our understanding of a different perspective."

ADOPT ROUTINES AND PROTOCOLS

Provision of tools and teacher modeling offer explicit instruction in the forming of dialogic questions. Creating the questions is but the first step. Equally as challenging to many students is practice in asking these questions to their classmates. Student-to-student questioning is an anomaly in most classrooms. Perhaps the most important reason for this is that students are not afforded the time and opportunity. Given the opportunity, however, few students seem to be comfortable spontaneously asking questions of one another in a whole class environment. Questioning a peer may not seem natural. Students may refrain from putting a peer on the spot, not wanting to embarrass or be embarrassed. While students naturally ask one another for help informally, they are less likely to enter into dialogue where there may be different perspectives. Structures can scaffold this asking, and routines and protocols are particularly helpful.

A Simple but Powerful Thinking Routine. Look back at Figure 6.1 and notice repetition of the prompt, *What makes you say that?* Ritchhart and colleagues (2011) researched the use of this question in K–12 schools and found it to be highly effective as a thinking routine. In their research, they compared the wording of this prompt to that of similar questions including *Why? What is your evidence? What reasons can you offer?* and so forth. They found *What makes you say that?* to be more open ended. The speaker could respond with either text-based or other evidence or by recounting the logic or reasoning used to reach a conclusion or answer. It also worked regardless of the perceived correctness of a response, appropriate for use with a right or a wrong answer. *What makes you say that?* was also perceived to be less threatening to a speaker than, for example, *Why?* The prompt is based upon the positive presupposition that the speaker has reasons for her comment or response.

Ritchhart and associates found that when teachers routinely use this prompt, students begin to ask one another, *What makes you say that?* This is an excellent beginning point for dialogical thinking and questioning—and one that can be taught to the youngest of our students. They also discovered that when this routine was used consistently, over time, students began embedding evidence for their responses in their initial statements and, as a result, their talk was extended and more complex. Both of these results promote desired outcomes of dialogue.

Ritchhart also notes that *What makes you say that?* is "as much a discourse routine as a thinking routine" (p. 165). Used as a follow-up question to a student statement lacking evidence or reasoning, this question prompts students to provide a basis for their claim. In Ritchhart's words, this question "goes a long way toward fostering a disposition toward evidential reasoning" and providing "an opportunity to consider multiple viewpoints or perspectives on a topic or idea" (p. 165).

Protocols That Provide Safe Structures. Protocols can scaffold increasingly complex dialogical thinking and questioning. They provide rules governing talk and set expectations for participation. This helps mitigate student discomfort with questioning a peer. Additionally, many protocols have built-in turn-taking, ensuring that all students have opportunity and responsibility for participation.

The Four A's. One text protocol, the Four A's, is particularly appropriate for fostering dialogue. Selection of an appropriate text is a key to the protocol's success in promoting true dialogue. One suggestion is that the text be somewhat ambiguous, open to multiple interpretations or responses or to a shared point of doubt about the meaning of the text (Haroutuniam-Gordon, 2014; McCann, 2014). Selection of suitable texts requires that teachers have deep knowledge of both their students and the text.

The protocol begins with individual and silent reading of a selected text. As students read the text, they identify passages that embody one *assumption* they believe the author holds, one idea with which they *agree*, an idea with which they could *argue*, and something to which they *aspire*. The critical thinking required to identify each of these Four A's prepares students to share their individual selections while peers listen to make meaning and compare them to their own. As students engage in the culminating dialogue, they interact with one another in a conversational manner, asking questions and building on others' thinking.

The Four A's not only scaffold speaking and listening, critical to effective dialogue, they also call for the kind of analytical thinking required for dialogic questioning. One of the primary skills associated with this type of questioning is "Ask questions to identify a speaker's assumptions (or beliefs)." This is a cognitively complex skill. Providing opportunities for students to question the assumptions of an author prepares them to ask questions to surface assumptions of others when in conversation about a range of topics. Likewise, identifying points of agreement and disagreement with a text and perhaps with one another's interpretation of the text affords practice in voicing and questioning differing perspectives.

The analysis and dialogue demanded by the Four A's supports student progression toward mastery of grade 6 through 12 curriculum standards. Identification of an author's assumption may be beyond the capacity of younger students; however, even "the littles" can learn to agree and respectfully disagree with others and provide reasons for so doing. This protocol can be modified to support the thinking and conversations of the youngest of our students.

Four A's Text Protocol

Select a short but rich text for students to read and analyze. Prior to their dialogue, students identify passages linked to their responses to the following questions:

- What *assumptions* does the author of the text hold?

- What do you *agree* with in the text?

- What do you want to *argue* with in the text?

- What parts of the text do you *aspire* to?

Create small groups of four, instructing students to name a facilitator and a timekeeper, both of whom will be full participants. Ask each group to identify a volunteer to go first. Proceed through four short rounds, providing the following instructions:

1. Round 1: The volunteer identifies one assumption, pointing to the location of the text that supports his choice. He will briefly talk about why he identified this assumption (up to one minute). The other participants listen actively but do not respond. If they would like to comment on what the speaker is saying, they take notes to use during the discussion round. Go around the quad until all members have had a turn to identify and discuss their assumptions.

2. Round 2: Another volunteer leads off by sharing one agreement, citing the text and talking about the reasons for her choice (up to one minute). As before, other members share their ideas and related textual evidence.

3. Round 3: During this round, a volunteer shares her argument, following the same procedures as with previous A's.

4. Round 4: The final round focuses on identified aspirations.

5. Discuss: Conclude the session with an open dialogue during which group members revisit the Four A's and compare their responses, seeking to find patterns. Encourage students to get behind one another's thinking, perhaps using the prompts provided in Figure 5.1. ■

Adapted from The National School Reform Faculty, schoolreforminitiative.org/doc/4_a_text.pdf.

Think-Pair-Share (TPS). A protocol that scaffolds student talk with one other student provides a good practice field for dialogic questioning. One widely used such protocol in K–12 is Think-Pair-Share. The thinking portion of the protocol occurs prior to assigning students to pairs. After silent thinking, they work individually or with a thinking partner to craft a question designed to get behind another's thinking about the focus area. Students use the Criteria for a Quality Dialogic Question (Figure 6.3) as they conceptualize and word their questions. Collaborative development of questions with a thinking partner, assuming the partners are carefully matched, can be productive. When students are able to talk through their thinking and say their questions aloud, they are better able to use the criteria to critique their work. After the thinking partners complete the crafting of their questions, they find different partners with whom to exchange questions.

During the "pair" segment of the protocol, students are instructed to ask their question of their assigned partners, provide time for thinking and responding, and pose follow-up questions to probe and extend. Each partner will have two minutes for posing her question, listening to another's response, paraphrasing when needed, and posing follow-up questions. The partners then switch roles. Teachers designate a Partner A and B (or 1 and 2, Peanut Butter and Jelly, Macaroni and Cheese, and so forth) to provide structure and accountability. During the first round, Partners A ask and Partners B respond; after two minutes, they switch roles. Teachers set clear expectations for questioning and active listening by the questioning partners and for complete responding by the one who is being questioned. It is important that this is not a "one-and-done" exercise, that the expectation is for continued dialogue throughout the two minutes allocated per partner.

Following exchange of questions with their "pair" partner, students return to their thinking partners with whom they worked to create their questions. They share their respective experiences and talk about how well their question worked, preparing to participate in whole-class sharing.

Interview Design (Speed Dating) is another protocol that can be used to structure students' asking of questions to their peers. This process enables students to pose their questions to multiple individuals and collect a range of responses, representing different perspectives.

Interview Design Process (Speed Dating)

1. Create interview lines.

   a. Have four students line up in straight lines with elbow room between them. (Note: You may choose to have different numbers of students in the lines—e.g., three facing three, five facing five, etc. I find that four is optimal, providing enough movement to afford students a rich experience but not so many interactions as to get "boring.")

   b. Then instruct four other students to form a facing row such that each person is facing one other individual.

   (Continued)

(Continued)

   c. Direct the remainder of students to line up in a similar fashion, with four facing four (making special provisions for "extra" students when class is not divisible by eight).

2. Designate one row in each set of paired rows as the moving row, the other as the stationary row.

3. Ask the individuals in the stationary row to pose their questions to the individual opposite them.

   a. They should listen carefully and jot down their partner's responses.

   b. Interviewers observe Think Time 2. At the end of an extended pause, they should ask a follow-up question to probe or extend the interviewee's thinking. The interviewer should refrain from expressing her own opinion, continuing to probe to get behind the partner's thinking.

   c. Afford two to three minutes for the first question-answer exchange. Then direct the partners to switch roles so that the original interviewer now becomes the responding partner and vice versa.

4. At the end of the two exchanges (four to six minutes), ask the individuals at the end of the row designated as the "moving" row to come to the head of their row. Everyone else shifts down one person so that they now face a new interview partner. Repeat the protocol.

5. After four rounds of questioning, each student examines all of the responses captured over the four rounds, looking for similarities and differences in thinking of peers. Each questioner should also reflect on how well their question worked, looking at the criteria. Prepare to share insights with the original partner.

6. After time for individual and pair reflection, the teacher leads a whole-class discussion focused on what students learned about dialogic questioning—what makes a good question, how best to ask, and so forth.

Note: The original version of this protocol uses teacher questions, oftentimes for the purpose of affording students an opportunity to think more deeply about issues, to review key ideas in a unit, and so forth. When used for this purpose, first-round questioners are asking one another the same question to get their thinking into the mix. The culminating stage groups all students with the same question together and has them synthesize responses across the class. When used as practice for dialogic questioning, a summary of responses is not appropriate. The idea, in this variation, is for students to practice listening to understand and questioning to clarify.■

Interview Design is a versatile protocol, one that can support student exchange of academic questions as well as student response to teacher questions. Michelle Shelton chose this protocol to provide students with practice in the use of dialogic questions to explore diverse points of view.

Student Questioners at Work

Michelle Shelton's students have created questions to prompt others' thinking about issues related to social injustices. Using the Interview Design protocol, each student poses their question to other classmates. After receiving an initial response, the questioners ask follow-up questions to identify assumptions and obtain a deeper understanding of respondents' comments. During a reflection following this activity, students identified interpretive listening to be an important feature of this protocol. They noted that they oftentimes don't really listen to others, particularly when talking about issues of disagreement. This exercise provided practice in listening which, together with the use of Think Time 2, enabled them to form follow-up questions that broadened their perspectives of the topic they had investigated. Video 6.3, "Dialogic Questioning Using Interview Design," illustrates how Interview Design scaffolded these student exchanges. ■

Socratic Seminars or Circles. The highest form of classroom dialogue is student driven. Student questions move the conversation forward, and teachers are primarily observers. This requires a high level of student skill and confidence. Socratic seminars or circles provide a structure that supports student skill development in this area. English teachers have been the most frequent users of seminars, but the structure can be adapted for all disciplines and for younger students.

Three primary teacher-controlled factors determine the effectiveness of a seminar: (1) selection of an appropriate text, (2) creation and maintenance of a safe environment, and (3) preparation of an initial focus question (Hale & City, 2006; Copeland, 2005; Roberts & Billings, 1999; Strong, M., 1997). Most models for seminars draw from the work of Mortimer Adler, whose book *The Paideia Proposal* (1982) provided a blueprint for seminars and made a strong argument for incorporating them into K–12 classrooms. The National Paideia Center (www.paideia .org) provides training and other resources to support practitioners committed to the instructional format.

Seminars require student preparation involving close reading of the assigned text, identification of passages related to the focus question, and creation of their own questions inspired by the text. As with other forms of dialogue, careful listening and adherence to norms related to respect and participation are required of all participants.

Socratic Circles and Seminars: Recommended Reading

A wide range of books offer specific structures and strategies to teachers wishing to hone their skills in preparing and facilitating this student-driven discussion. Two of my favorites are appropriate for all content areas and grade levels.

Middle school teacher Matt Copeland offers practical advice for planning and preparing students for participation in what he calls Socratic Circles, an inside-outside version of a seminar. His book *Socratic Circles: Fostering Critical and Creative Thinking in Middle and High School* (2005) draws from his years of refining this approach with his middle school students.

Although his experience is in the middle school English classroom, the strategies are highly adaptable to other instructional settings.

The Teacher's Guide to Leading Student-Centered Discussions (2006) by Michael Hale and Elizabeth City is another very practical approach to designing student-driven dialogue. These authors provide a four-dimensional framework for decision-making about seminars. The dimensions—safety, authentic participation, challenge, and ownership—offer teachers a way to think about supporting students in developing the capacity to benefit fully from the seminar experience. ■

Seminars move students beyond one-on-one dialogue provided in Think-Pair-Share and Interview Design to a large group setting in which they are challenged to listen carefully to multiple peers and work collaboratively using questions and responses to construct a web that widens and deepens understanding for each individual member.

INCORPORATE INTO DAILY LESSONS

Like other types of student questions, those inviting dialogue do not usually emerge spontaneously during a daily lesson. Teachers design lessons with an eye to appropriate points at which dialogue could advance learning, and they are intentional in adopting a dialogic stance as they enact their lessons.

Dialogue serves important purposes within an instructional cycle, but as McCann (2014) observes, dialogues differ from point to point in lessons, serving different functions. The nature of the dialogue "depends on the structures and expectations that the teacher, as the orchestrator for learning, establishes" (p. 79). If student questions are to drive the dialogue, teacher expectations and structures must advance this end.

Take, for example, a geometry lesson planned by Jarid Moore for his eighth-grade students (featured in Video 4.1). He strategically integrated opportunities for student dialogic questions at three points in the lesson. The first occurred at the beginning of the lesson following individual solutions of a problem designed to review and activate the prior day's learning. Mr. Moore instructed students to exchange solution paths with their assigned partners. Partners A initiated the talk, each explaining the strategies used to solve the problem. Partners B listened actively and asked dialogic questions to get behind their partners' thinking. After several minutes, the teacher, who had been monitoring pair talk to obtain feedback, instructed the partners to switch roles, with Partners B sharing their approaches. Listening in to these students, observers noted the extent to which the student questions led to deeper dialogue about alternative ways to attack the problem.

About midway through this class, Mr. Moore instructed partners to work collaboratively on a new problem that involved transfer of learning to a real-life situation. As they worked toward a solution, partners around the room engaged in lively dialogue as they tried out different approaches. The conversations were peppered with questions that drove the conversations and problem-solving forward. After time for pair work, the teacher combined pairs into preassigned quads. The task was for pairs to compare their approaches, digging deeper into geometric understandings. Questions continued to flourish around the room.

As the lesson moved to its culmination, Mr. Moore invited the students to engage in whole-class dialogue. During this phase of the lesson, students spoke to one another, offering explanations and asking questions. They did not raise their hands but entered into the conversation in an authentic and unprompted manner. They afforded one another think time as they compared approaches and built on one another's ideas.

This student-driven class did not resemble my geometry class of years gone by during which my teacher methodically presented theorems and solved problems while we compliant students watched and took notes. My teacher was the lead actor in our class; Mr. Moore was the designer and orchestrator of his students' learning. He utilized simple structures and protocols, pair talk followed by quad sharing and collaborative dialogue. As his students moved through this lesson, they used questions to assess and affirm surface knowledge but more significantly, to take their understanding deeper.

Two of the primary purposes of dialogue are to move students from surface to deep learning and to facilitate learning how to learn (Nottingham et al., 2017). The use of dialogic questioning in this geometry class accomplished both of these purposes.

Student dialogic questions leverage engagement and deepen learning. Our job as teachers is to determine the points in a lesson to facilitate this process through the use of appropriate structures and learning tasks.

MAKE TIME AND SPACE

Tools and strategies scaffold student preparation of questions, and protocols afford a structure for practice. The ultimate goal, of course, is for students to develop the facility to form questions in real time during class and the confidence to insert themselves into the flow of a lesson to pose their questions. Learning to ask dialogic questions is an important life skill that can be honed through authentic classroom talk.

To enable fluid, dynamic dialogue during which students speak to one another, agreeing and disagreeing and asking questions to surface and understand different perspectives, we must be willing to change the nature and rhythm of classroom talk. As Dillon (1994) argued, if we want students to ask questions, we teachers must stop asking them! This creates the space for student questions. Again, the most important source of time for student questions comes during the pauses following comments (Think Time 2). The students in Mr. Moore's geometry class had learned the importance of this time to process and decide upon a question or a comment. They provided this time to one another and, without raising hands, listened and waited, did not interrupt, and thereby constructed deeper understandings.

AFFORD PRACTICE WITH FEEDBACK

While monitoring student interactions, both in dialogues structured by protocols and in free-flowing discussions, teachers provide both reinforcing and constructive feedback based upon established criteria. More effective is the planning of opportunities for self-assessment and peer feedback. Providing students with standards for assessment, such as the criteria presented in Figure 6.3, enables them to assess quality and use of these questions for dialogue.

The Fishbowl is a protocol that can be utilized to facilitate peer feedback. While students in the inside circle engage in dialogue, with the expectation that they use dialogic questions to promote multiple purposes, students in the outside circle listen and take notes related to specified expectations (Copeland, 2005). Some teachers charge those in the outside circle with listening to all discussants and mapping the flow of the conversation. At the end of the round, members of the outside circle provide feedback to the inside circle. Other teachers instruct each student in the outside circle to track the questions and engagement of one peer, usually the one whom they are sitting behind. When the latter strategy is used, observers provide one-on-one feedback to the discussants prior to the teacher facilitating a whole-class discussion about the strengths and areas for growth of the process. Whichever variation is used, the process of observing to provide feedback benefits both the discussants and the observers.

Enhancing student skill in dialogic questioning is a process that occurs over time. Intentionality in the design and operation of a feedback loop is particularly critical to growth and improvement of student questioning in the context of dialogue.

INVITE STUDENT REFLECTION

Whereas feedback provides criterion-referenced information on progress in developing identified skills, reflection engages the individual learner in thinking about experiences so as to learn from them. Both are important. Learning to ask dialogic questions involves as much a change in individual attitudes and behaviors as skill in forming the questions. For this reason, reflection serves as an important tool for students to surface factors affecting their willingness to pose these questions.

A useful structure for supporting this reflection is Reflective Questioning. This begins with individual thinking and writing in response to prompts provided by the teacher. Prompts might include the following:

What encourages or motivates you to ask dialogic questions that help you get behind someone's comments and thinking?

What keeps you from asking questions to get behind your classmates' comments or ways of thinking about a topic?

What might we do as a class to encourage one another to ask and respond to these kinds of questions?

Following time for written responses to these or similar prompts, students work in triads to support one another in deeper reflection. Over the course of three rounds, each student has the opportunity to talk out loud about his reflection while a second student asks questions to take the reflection deeper. A third student observes silently, taking note of what the interviewer said and did to take the speaker's thinking deeper. The observer provides feedback to the speaker and interviewer at the end of the round. Students switch roles after each three- to four-minute round of talk so that each one has the opportunity (1) to engage in personal reflection, (2) to question a peer to promote deeper reflection, and (3) to observe and provide feedback. At the conclusion of three rounds, the teacher leads the class in a debrief focused on what they learned from participation in this reflection.

Reflective Questioning

During each of the three rounds, group members rotate through each of the following roles:

1. **Speaker/Reflector**: Talk openly about your reflections—exploring the relationship between your beliefs and your behaviors. Respond to the questions asked by the interviewer in a thoughtful manner.

2. **Interviewer**:

   a. Ask the speaker questions that encourage her to reflect more deeply. Two categories of questions are appropriate:

   i. Probing questions

   (1) *To clarify*—for example, *"What do you mean when you say . . . ?"* **OR** *"Help me get behind your thinking. . . ."*

   (2) *To seek greater specificity*—for example, *"Can you give me an example of. . . ?"* **OR** *"Talk about a time when you were able to. . . ."*

   (3) *To encourage completeness*—for example, *"Say more about. . . ."* **OR** *"You've told me about how you hope to. . . . Talk a bit about how you. . . ."*

   (4) *To seek evidence or a rationale*—for example, *"What makes you say that?" "Do you have evidence to support this claim?"*

   ii. Reflective questions

   (1) *"What data or evidence support this conclusion . . . ?"* **or** *"How did you reach this conclusion?"*

   (2) *"What if . . . ?"*

   (3) *"Why do you think . . . ?"*

   (4) *"Talk to me about what success might look like."*

   (5) *"Imagine that you. . . ."*

   (6) *"Call to mind a time when. . . ."*

   (7) *"Let's assume for a minute that. . . ."*

   (8) *"What might be the relationship between . . . and . . . ?"*

   b. Your role is to listen intently, probing gently when necessary, and to assist the reflector in more fully surfacing ideas. You should attempt to listen at two levels:

   i. Active Listening—listening for content and ideas

   ii. Empathic Listening—listening for feelings and emotions

3. **Observer**: Look for evidence of deep and reflective thought.

   a. Questions: What did the interviewer say? What questions did he or she ask that seemed to prompt reflective thought?

   b. Nonverbal: What about the interviewer's manner seemed to facilitate reflection (e.g., facial expressions, eye movement, gesturing, tone of voice, etc.)?■

Periodic engagement in reflective questioning not only provides students with the chance to reflect deeply on progress in dialogic questioning, it also affords practice in questioning itself. The prompts driving the reflection can be changed to serve a variety of instructional purposes, including deepening understanding of content knowledge.

In Closing: *Changing the Equation*

Developing student capacity as dialogic questioners will transform student learning. Rather than passively responding to teacher questions or even posing an occasional question of their own, students interact with one another to take learning deeper and develop understanding of other perspectives. This class dynamic empowers individuals while building a community of learners.

The transformation begins with a shift in teacher role, from director to designer and orchestrator of learning experiences. This requires that teachers relinquish control over every move of talk and commit to developing student skills and will to assume responsibility for their own learning. Many students are reticent to assume this new role. Knowing that this radical change is a journey, not an event, teachers and students alike need to exercise patience, persistence, and grace throughout the transition.

The dividends affect the short term—increased student learning and achievement—and the long term—enhanced ability to understand different perspectives and engage in dialogue that supports healthier relationships in one's personal life and contributes to a stronger democratic society. The incentives for choosing this course have never been greater. The quality of our students' lives are at stake.

Begin with the end in mind. The purpose of dialogic questions in the online environment is the same as when face-to-face: to enable students to get behind another's thinking, particularly when it differs from their own or from the norm. When students are working remotely, these opportunities are less likely to occur naturally and need to be more carefully orchestrated. An important consideration for teachers of young children is the identification of "just right" goals for these learners, especially in the online environment. Teaching "littles" to respectfully question to understand and respectfully agree and disagree is an important goal and can be addressed by selecting age-appropriate strategies and structures to support student interactions.

Highlight the appropriate mindframe, skills, and tools for students in the lesson where particular question types will be emphasized. Forming and asking questions that challenge another's thinking in a productive and tactful manner is harder to do when not face-to-face. Students may be less willing to risk confronting another for fear of being misunderstood. This makes it even more important to develop a community norm around the mindframe, *I ask questions to understand other perspectives and to engage in collaborative thinking and learning.* A mini-lesson focused on the scaffolding of sample prompts and stems, Figure 6.1, can bolster the success of student preparation for and engagement in a dialogue where they are expected to pose questions.

Strategically position formal requests for dialogic questions in the unit or lesson. Planned opportunities for dialogue are most productive when students have developed sufficient surface knowledge to be able to form personal perspectives. They are then prepared to go deeper in learning and integrate and transfer understandings to their personal realities. Selection of a "third point" for dialogue, a carefully identified source (e.g., a piece of literature, an historical document, an editorial, a videotaped commentary), is prerequisite to students preparing questions that meet the criteria offered in Figure 6.3.

Adapt protocols and response routines for online use. All of the protocols presented in this chapter can be modified for online use. For example, the Four A's provide a structure for creation of a purposeful question following analysis of a reading. Inside-Outside Circles can be adapted for virtual use as can Interview Design and Reflective Questioning.

Dialogue itself best occurs in a synchronous environment that allows students to interact with one another in real time. It can also be orchestrated in written form on a discussion board. When using a discussion board for student dialogue, create expectations for both the formatting of questions posed and the responses offered. Regarding postings, Boettcher (Boettcher & Conrad, 2016) recommends a "three-part post," using a "what, why, and what I wish" statement

(p. 159). Adapted to the posting of dialogic questions, this would require the questioner to accompany the question itself with a statement of the importance of the question (the why) and hopes for responses (e.g., open, honest, divergent opinions). Expectations for responses to questions traditionally require that each student respond at least two times.

When using the discussion board to support a true dialogue, this quantitative requirement is not sufficient. While rubrics for responses vary by age and content area, common to all are (1) taking a position on the issue raised by the question, (2) supporting one's view with evidence (from text when possible), (3) elaborating on one's position with a multisentence, not a three-to-five-word, comment, (4) staying on topic, (5) connecting one's response to a comment made by earlier respondents so that threads are woven throughout the conversation, and (6) weaving real-life examples into responses as appropriate.

Carefully select a limited number of tech tools (i.e., platforms and apps) for use by a class of students. A number of previously mentioned apps can support student testing and refinement of their dialogic questions. Flipgrid, for example, enables questioners to ask aloud and listen critically to peer responses to determine how the question "worked." Students might also present their questions in this space and provide feedback to one another (using the established criteria). Younger students can also use SeeSaw or Dojo for similar purposes. The most appropriate virtual space for dialogue occurs in a synchronous learning platform such as Zoom or Google Meet, especially within breakout rooms for students with the maturity to work independently (with occasional teacher stop bys) in such setting.∎

Curtain Call: Revisiting Key Ideas

KEY IDEAS	QUESTIONS FOR PERSONAL REFLECTION
1. When students ask and answer dialogic questions, they increase their academic performance and learn how to engage in democratic processes.	• Speculate as to why student engagement in asking and answering questions of one another might contribute to academic achievement. • In what ways do you think the ability to ask questions to better understand others' perspectives might contribute to effective citizenship?
2. Mindframe for dialogic questioning: *I ask questions to understand other perspectives and to engage in collaborative thinking and learning.*	• To what extent do your students ask questions of peers with whom they disagree? • How often do your students engage in dialogue that results in learning from one another and building on one another's ideas?
3. The five skills listed in Figure 6.1 require students to actively engage in analyzing their own and others' assumptions.	• How proficient are your students in using these identified skills as they engage in conversation with one another? • In what ways can you imagine using this figure as a resource to support student skill development?
4. Students can use the Criteria for a Quality Dialogic Question (Figure 6.3) as a single-point rubric to write and assess dialogic questions.	• Under what circumstances might you ask your students to use this tool? • How, if at all, would you modify this tool to fit your subject area and grade level?
5. *What makes you say that?* is an effective thinking routine to support dialogue.	• When and how might you introduce this prompt to your students? • How might you reinforce and encourage its use?
6. Protocols scaffold student development of skills in dialogic questioning.	• Which of the protocols introduced in this chapter—Pair Talk, Interview Design, Socratic Seminar—have you used in the past? Which will you consider experimenting with in the future? • What other protocols or strategies might you adapt for use in developing student capacity to engage in dialogic questioning and responding?
7. Dialogic questioning promotes different instructional purposes and can be effectively used at various points in a learning cycle.	• For what purposes are you most interested in increasing your use of this type of student question? • What factors will you consider as you plan increased opportunities for your students to form and ask dialogic questions?
8. Feedback and reflection are keys for increasing student proficiency in dialogic questioning.	• What approaches to feedback do you believe will work best with your students? • What might be the value of adapting reflective questioning for use by your students?

CHAPTER 7

The End in Mind

*Increased Agency Within and
Beyond the Classroom*

Krista Mintz and Britton Young reflect on their experiences in developing their students' skills as questioners. They draw from their experiences in the mathematics and science classrooms as well as from their role as coaches of student robotics and green car teams. The latter setting affords them opportunities to observe students applying cognitive skills, including questioning, in live, high-stakes settings. In this brief excerpt, Video 7.1, "Teachers Dialogue About Power of Student Questions," they talk about how their students use all four forms of questions as they collaborate in design, production, and operation of award-winning robots and green cars.▪

Individuals who are competent and confident questioners approach new and unknown situations with a certain degree of self-reliance, a belief they can successfully inquire into the unfamiliar, and confidence they will find a pathway forward. Evidence of the need for this abounds in the summer of 2020, the year of the COVID-19 pandemic, as I am writing the final pages of this book.

"Agency describes our capacity to act in empowered and autonomous ways. Beliefs about our agency influence confidence and contribute to our resiliency." (Fisher, Frey, & Smith, 2019, p. 20)

A few cases in point. Researchers are exploring alternative ways of controlling this virus by accelerating development of vaccines and treatments. Educators are engaging in deep dialogue as they seek to balance students' academic, social-emotional, and physical well-being during months of uncertainty. Ordinary citizens, seeking to maneuver uncharted territories in their daily lives, use questions to seek information required for problem-solving and decision-making. And those who are successfully creating a new normal in their personal lives are relying upon metacognitive processes to control and monitor daily activities.

The capacity to form the right questions enables individuals of all walks of life to thrive, not just survive, during these times of uncertainty.

The capacity to form the right questions enables individuals of all walks of life to thrive, not just survive, during these times of uncertainty. This capacity contributes to one's agency or sense of control over the future. Agency relates to self-confidence, self-efficacy, growth mindset, perseverance, grit, and resiliency—dispositions we seek to develop in all learners (Fisher et al., 2019). This is a vision for all of our students: They are developing skills and dispositions as questioners that equip them to act, not react, in challenging times and to thrive regardless of what is happening in their external environments.

BEYOND SCAFFOLDING—
TOWARD A HOLISTIC APPROACH

The intent of this book is to provide a manual of practice for teachers and students, a framework and resources to support advancement in using four types of questions. To further this end, each question type has been considered separately, a chapter dedicated to each. In practice, however, these question types are interrelated. They feed off of one another, a self-question leading to an academic one, the academic one inspiring an exploratory one, the exploratory one resulting in dialogical exchanges, and so on. The question types are fluid and dynamic, not fragmented and mechanical. They are powerful when used by all, young and old alike, to proactively approach the world around us.

Because of the belief that student questions don't emerge spontaneously in most classrooms, this book positions "teachers as activators" and uses an eight-part process for development of the four different question types. This may appear to be a formulistic approach to the development of student capacity. In practice, this process, like all

FIGURE 7.1 Types of Questions

Self

Academic

Exploratory

Dialogic

FIGURE 7.2 Process for Developing Student Capacity as Questioners

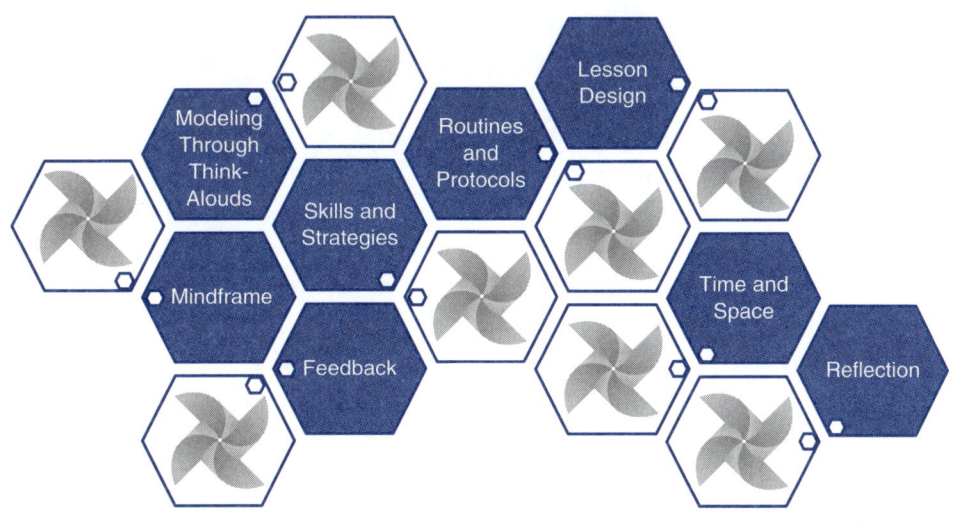

Modeling Through Think-Alouds

Skills and Strategies

Routines and Protocols

Lesson Design

Mindframe

Feedback

Time and Space

Reflection

of teaching, is fluid and depends upon teacher style, preference, and response to different learner needs and characteristics.

INTEGRATED, NOT ISOLATED

The Taxonomy of Student Questions is a framework for thinking about the purposes of questions in different contexts. Students can benefit from developing a vocabulary to talk about questions. They also profit from knowing that differing situations call for different types of questions. As students become conversant with the four categories and confident in their use of each of these types of questions, teachers can assist them in understanding the interconnections between and among these. In practice, skilled questioners draw on each to weave a web of questions that deepen and strengthen their understanding of the world around them.

When students ask questions, they can transform surface encounters and superficial responses into deeper understandings of the complexity of ideas, other people, and themselves. Valuing and using metacognitive or self-questions result in more measured and reasonable responses to new situations and life issues. Ask students to think of self-questions as the center point of a web of questions and correspondent understandings. Help them understand that without a center point, the web cannot be formed. When they do not assume an internal stance of self-questioning, they will not engage inquisitively with their environment.

The relationship of the other question types to one another is reciprocal and supportive. Academic questions, which focus on acquiring information or building a knowledge base, can lead to or result from an exploratory or a dialogic question. Learning about an issue (academic) may lead to wondering about a new way of approaching it (exploratory) or to a question that engages others in talking about different perspectives or interpretations (dialogic). Likewise, an authentic wondering (exploratory question) might lead one to ask academic questions to build a sound knowledge base or to ask questions to determine others' perspectives (dialogic). Finally, dialogic questions invite others to offer background knowledge to support a perspective or serve to generate collaborative thinking that leads to mutually created exploratory questions.

> When students ask questions, they can transform surface encounters and superficial responses into deeper understandings of the complexity of ideas, other people, and themselves.

These three question types operate in tandem, each type seamlessly spawning another. No one is of greater value than another. Dialogic questions sometimes require more tact and courage to ask, and exploratory questions usually result from more out-of-the-box, creative thinking. This does not make them better, only of a different order.

The ultimate goal is to encourage students to approach their learning and their lives from a position of questioning rather than passive receiving or reacting. This necessitates use of questions from each of our four categories and an understanding of the connections between and among these.

> The ultimate goal is to encourage students to approach their learning and their lives from a position of questioning rather than passive receiving or reacting.

Even as all types of questions are connected, so should the teaching of skills and dispositions be integrated into ongoing instruction. When students form questions about content under study, they engage in making meaning of a reading, a visual, or an auditory input. Forming a question requires students to first analyze content and then to create their inquiry. Asking questions is an integral part of curriculum, not something separate and apart.

FLUID, NOT FORMULISTIC

Yet this still leaves many teachers concerned about the time required to cover all that is expected and wondering how to integrate one more thing into an already full agenda. Where, you may ask, do I begin? How do I proceed?

The primary challenge is changing student beliefs regarding their role and responsibilities, helping them understand that asking is as important as answering. As argued throughout, this begins with a focus on mindframes. The concept of mindframe is similar to the notion of disposition, which Costa and Kallick (2014) define as "tendencies toward particular patterns of intellectual behavior" (p. 1). In the book *10 Mindframes for Visible Learning* (Hattie & Zierer, 2017), Hattie popularized the term *mindframes*, defining them as "how [teachers] think about their tasks," and why they do what they do rather than relying upon "moment-by-moment decision making" (p. xiv). So it is with the concept of mindframes for students.

The idea behind the student mindframes is to challenge learners' ways of thinking about how they do the task of learning; to convey the expectation that questioning, not just answering, should be their approach; and to specify the why for each of the question types. The hope is that over time, students will internalize these ways of thinking so that asking questions becomes

> The hope is that over time, students will internalize these ways of thinking so that asking questions becomes an automatic, not a mechanical or forced, response.

an automatic, not a mechanical or forced, response. The mindframes advocate for proactive, not passive, learners who become naturally inclined to inquire, not reflexively accept information transmitted to them.

Student adoption of these mindframes supports practice over time in forming and asking questions and, with practice, increased proficiency in the area. Teachers continue to be intentional in designing lessons that capitalize on student questions and in affording time and space for them to emerge organically. However, intensive scaffolding is no longer required because students own this role in the classroom. Mindframes are the gateway to this transformation.

While nurturing this transformation, teachers can draw from the resources provided to structure and reinforce skill development and confidence.

REALIZING THE POTENTIAL— IN SCHOOL AND BEYOND

Empowering students as questioners is personal to me. When my son Will was 10, he came home from school one day very upset. When I asked what was bothering him, he looked at me with tears in his eyes and said, "She pointed her finger at me today and said, 'Will, you have one more question to ask today. So it had better be a good one!'" I talked with Will about his questioning in class, and he said, "I ask questions when I don't understand, or when I wonder about something." I assured him that his dad and I were proud of his thinking and valued his questions. I made an appointment with the teacher and had a heart-to-heart conversation during which I asked her if Will's questions were relevant, if they were serious. She responded, "Well, yes, but sometimes his questions slow me down, and I have science to teach." I explained that Will had always been encouraged to question, that we believed this was the best way to learn. I left the conference wondering if I had been clear, yet tactful. To my knowledge, Will continued to ask his questions. On his final report card for the year, the teacher wrote, "Will has been a leader this year in helping other students understand." I smiled, realizing that I had effectively communicated and that this teacher apparently had understood.

> "Students have every good reason but one not to ask the questions that occur to them. That one reason is mastery of the world through knowledge and understanding. For the purpose of asking a question eventuates in learning."
> (Dillon, 1988, p. 17)

Ron Berger (2014) writes persuasively of students becoming leaders of their own learning. He is a strong advocate for student-engaged assessment that focuses on building "the independence, critical thinking skills, perseverance, and self-reflective understanding students need for college and careers" (p. 5). The ability to ask questions underpins each of these outcomes. When asked about the value of forming and asking their own questions, students almost always mention a sense of empowerment and ownership of their learning. My son Will was a leader of his own learning, in school and beyond. I wish this for all of our young people.

In the closing years of the twentieth century, many thought leaders raised the alarm about business as usual in our classrooms, warning that passive learning was not preparing students for the 21st century. Murnane and Levy (1996) made the case for teaching students to ask their own questions, claiming that this would not only pay dividends in school but also equip them to participate more fully in building a strong economy and a vibrant democratic society. Almost twenty years later, in *Dancing With Robots: Human Skills for Computerized Work* (Levy & Murnane, 2016), these thought leaders continued their challenge to schools to develop skills that are required in a new economic reality. Their analysis of current and emerging jobs revealed two prevailing tasks: "solving unstructured problems" and "working with new information." These are best accomplished by those who have learned how to ask questions, not respond passively to those raised by others.

Student Questioners at Work

The eighth graders who spoke of the value of question-asking to their learning in the video that opened this book (Video 1.1) also foresee this skill to be an important one for their future success. In Video 7.2, "Students Relate Their Future Success to the Ability to Ask Questions," they share with one another their future aspirations as business owners, engineers, and perhaps even U.S. president! They talk about ways in which they believe their skills as questioners will support their life goals. These young students recognize the potential value of questioning to extend far beyond their school days. They wisely intuit that skills as questioners will empower them to exercise greater control over the course of their lives. ▪

Developing student capacity to thrive in the classroom and beyond is part of what motivates teachers to continue their own learning and growth. Teachers committed to this goal see the value in adopting and consistently acting upon the mindframe, *I am intentional in nurturing students as questioners.* To this end, they embrace these questions as they engage with each new class of students.

- *What knowledge and **skills** do my students need to be effective questioners?*

- *How can I help my students develop the **will**, the frames of mind, to form and ask questions to advance their learning?*

- *How can I partner with my students in developing a classroom culture where they can experience the **thrill** of learning by asking and answering their own questions?*

It is my hope that this book will motivate and support you in this journey and contribute to unlocking the unlimited potential that resides within each one of our children by developing their skill, will, and thrill as questioners.

References

Adler, M. (1982). *The Paideia proposal*. New York: Macmillan.

Alexander, R. (2020). *A dialogic teaching companion*. New York: Routledge.

Almarode, J. T., Fisher, D., Frey, N., & Hattie, J. (2018). *Visible learning for science, grades K–12: What works best to optimize student learning*. Thousand Oaks, CA: Corwin.

Alvermann, D. E. (2004, January). Multiliteracies and self-questioning in the service of science learning. *ResearchGate*. https://www.researchgate.net/publication/239924639_-

Asik, G., Aydin, E., & Erktin, E. (2015). Fostering self-questioning to improve mathematical word problem-solving. Paper presented at European Educational Research Association, September 20, 2015.

Bandura, A. (2011). Social cognitive theory. In P. A. M. van Lange, A. W. Kruglanski, & E. T. Higgins (Eds.). *Handbook of social psychological theories* (pp. 349–373). Thousand Oaks, CA: Sage.

Barell, J. (2003). *Developing more curious minds*. Alexandria, VA: ASCD.

Barnette, J., Orletsky, S., Sattes, B., & Walsh, J. (1995, April). Wait-time: Effective and trainable. Paper presented at the annual meeting of the American Educational Research Association, San Francisco, CA. ERIC Document Reproduction Service No. ED383706.

Berger, R. (2014). *Leaders of their own learning: Student-engaged assessment*. San Francisco: Jossey-Bass.

Berger, W. (2014). *A more beautiful question*. New York: Bloomsbury.

Berger, W. (2018, December 12). Ask these questions and your boss might just promote you. *Psychology Today*. http://tiny.cc/0yxlpz.

Berger, W., & Foster E. (2020). *Beautiful questions in the classroom: Transforming classrooms into cultures of curiosity and inquiry*. Thousand Oaks, CA: Corwin Press.

Berkeley, S. Marshak, L. Mastropieri, M. A., & Scruggs, T. E. (2010). Improving student comprehension of social studies text: A self-questioning strategy for inclusive middle school classes. *Remedial and Special Education*, *32*(2), 105–113.

Berry, J. W., & Chew, S. L. (2008). Improving learning through interventions of student-generated questions and concept maps. *Teaching of Psychology*, *35*(4), 305–312.

Boettcher, J., & Conrad, R. (2016). *The online teaching survival guide: Simple and practical pedagogical tools* (2nd ed.). San Francisco: Jossey Bass.

Bransford, J. D., Brown, J. L., & Cocking, R. R. (Eds.). (2000). *How people learn: Brain, mind, experience, and school*. Committee on Development of the Sciences of Learning and Committee on Learning Research and Educational Practice. Washington, DC: National Academy Press.

Brown, A. L., & Campione, J. C. (1998). Designing a community of young learners: Theoretical and practical lessons. In N. M. Lambert & B. C. McCombs (Eds.). *How students learn: Reforming schools through learner-centered education* (pp. 153–186). Washington, DC: American Psychological Association.

Cazden, C. B. (2001). *Classroom discourse: The language of teaching and learning*. Portsmouth, NH: Heinemann.

Chin, C. (2001, April). Student-generated questions: What they tell us about students' thinking. Paper presented at the annual meeting of the American Educational Research Association, Seattle.

Cocking, R. R., Brown, A. L., & Branford, J. D. (2000). *How people learn: Brain, mind, experience and school*. Washington, DC: National Academies Press.

Common Core State Standards Initiative. (2020). *English language arts standards: Speaking & listening: Grade 2*. www.corestandards.org/ELA-Literacy/SL/2/

Conley, D. T. (2005). *College knowledge: What it really takes for students to succeed and what we can do to get them ready*. San Francisco: Jossey-Bass.

Copeland, M. (2005). *Socratic circles: Fostering critical and creative thinking in middle and high school*. Portland, ME: Stenhouse Press.

Costa, A., & Kallick, B. (2014). *Dispositions: Reframing teaching and learning*. Thousand Oaks, CA: Corwin.

Dewey, J. (2013). Democracy and education: An introduction to the philosophy of education. CreateSpace Independent Publishing Platform. USA: CreateSpace.

Dillon, J. T. (1988). *Questioning and teaching: A manual of practice*. New York: Teachers College Press.

Dillon, J. T. (1994). *Using discussion in classrooms*. Philadelphia, PA: Open University Press.

Doukmak, R. (2014, Spring). Are you sure you don't have any questions? Dialogic teaching as a way to promote students' questions. *ELTED, 16*.

Engel, J. S. (1988). Students questioning students (SQS): A technique to invite students' involvement. *Gifted Education International, 5*, 179–185.

Engel, S. (2015). *The hungry mind: The origins of curiosity in childhood*. Cambridge, MA: Harvard University Press.

Fisher, D., Frey, N., & Hattie, J. (2020). *Distance learning playbook, grades K–12: Teaching for engagement & impact in any setting*. Thousand Oaks, CA: Corwin.

Frey, N., Fisher, D., & Smith, D. (2019). *All learning is social and emotional: Helping students develop essential skills for the classroom and beyond*. Alexandria, VA: ASCD.

Frey, N., Hattie, J., & Fisher, D. (2018). *Developing assessment-capable visible learners, grades K–12: Maximizing skill, will, and thrill*. Thousand Oaks, CA: Corwin Press.

Fullan, M., Quinn J., & McEachen, J. (2018). *Deep learning: Engage the world, change the world*. Thousand Oaks, CA: Corwin Press.

Gall, M. (1970). The use of questions in teaching. *Review of Educational Research, 40*, 707–721.

Good, T. L., & Brophy, J. E. (1991). *Looking in classrooms* (5th ed.). New York: HarperCollins Publisher.

Goodwin, B. (2018). *Out of curiosity: Restoring the power of hungry minds for better schools, workplaces, and lives*. Denver, CO: McRel International.

Goodwin, B. (2020). *Building a curious school: Restore the joy that brought you to school*. Thousand Oaks, CA: Corwin Press.

Hale, M. S., & City, E. A. (2006). *Leading student-centered discussions: Talking about texts in the classroom.* Thousand Oaks, CA: Corwin Press.

Haller, E. P., Child, D. A., & Walberg, H. J. (1988). Can comprehension be taught? A quantitative synthesis of "metacognitive" students. *Educational Researcher, 17*(9), 5–8.

Haroutuniam-Gordon, S. (2014). *Interpretive discussion: Engaging students in text-based discussions.* Cambridge, MA: Harvard University Press.

Hattie, J. (2009). *Visible learning: A synthesis of 800+ meta-analyses related to achievement.* New York: Routledge.

Hattie, J. (2012). *Visible learning for teachers: Maximizing learning.* New York: Routledge.

Hattie, J., & Donoghue, G. (2016). Learning strategies: A synthesis and conceptual model. *NPJ Science Learn 1,* 16013. https://doi.org/10.1038/npjscilearn.2016.13

Hattie, J., & Yates, G. (2014). *Visible learning and the science of how we learn.* New York: Routledge.

Hattie, J., & Zierer, K. (2017). *10 mindframes for visible learning: Teaching for success.* New York: Routledge.

Hunkins, E. F. (1995). *Teaching thinking through effective questioning.* Boston, MA: Christopher-Gordon.

Israel, S. E., Block, C. C., Bauserman, K. L., & Kinnucan-Welsch, K. (2005). Self-assessment strategies for middle school student readers. In S. E. Israel, C. C. Block, K. L. Bauserman, & K. Kinnucan-Welsch (Eds.), *Metacognition in literacy learning: Theory, assessment, instruction, and professional development* (p. 143). Mahwah, NJ: Lawrence Erlbaum.

Juzwik, M. M., Borsheim-Black, C., Caughlan, S., & Heintz, A. (2013). *Inspiring dialogue: Talking to learn in the English classroom.* New York: Teachers College Press.

Kashdan, T., Disabato, D., Goodman, F., & Mcknight, P. (2019). *The five-dimensional curiosity scale revised (5DCR): Briefer subscales while separating general overt and covert social curiosity.* https://doi.org/10.31219/osf.io/pu8f3

Kazemi, E., & Hintz, A. (2014). *Intentional talk: How to structure and lead productive mathematical discussions.* Portland, ME: Stenhouse Publishers.

Leslie, I. (2004). *Curious: The desire to know and why your future depends on it.* New York: Basic Books.

Levy, F., & Murnane, R. J. (2013). *Dancing with robots: Human skills for computerized work.* Washington, DC: Third Way.

Livio, M. (2017). *Why? What makes us curious?* New York: Simon & Schuster.

Loewenstein, G. (1994). The psychology of curiosity: A review and reinterpretation. *Psychology Bulletin, 116*(1), 75–98.

MacKenzie, T. (2018). *Inquiry mindset: Nurturing the dreams, wonders, and curiosities of our youngest learners.* EdTechTeam.

Matibag-Angeles, H. (2016). Input modification and self-questioning: Effect on level 7 students' comprehension of science texts. Presented at 2016 CELC Symposium, pp. 155–163. https://nus.edu/2Wz2ytp

McCann, T. M. (2014). *Transforming talk into text: Argument writing, inquiry, and discussion, grades 6–12.* New York: Teachers College Press.

Mehan, H. (1979). *Learning lessons: Social organization in the classroom.* Cambridge, MA: Harvard University Press.

Mercer, N., & Dawes, L. (2008). The value of exploratory talk. In N. Mercer & S. Hodgkinson (Eds.), *Exploring talk in school* (55–72). London: Routledge.

Minigan, A. P. (2017, May 24). The importance of curiosity and questions in 21st century learning. *Education Week*, *36*(32).

Mohr, K. A. J. (1998). Teacher talk: A summary analysis of effective teachers' discourse during primary literacy lessons. *Journal of Classroom Interaction*, *33*(2), 16–23.

Murnane, R. J., & Levy, F. (1996). *Teaching the new basic skills: Principals for educating children in a changing economy*. New York: Basic Books.

National Academies of Science-Engineering-Medicine. (2018). *How people learn II: Learners, contexts, and cultures*. Washington, DC: The National Academics Press.

National Institute of Child and Human Development. (2000). *Report of the national reading panel. Teaching children to read: An evidence-based assessment of the scientific research literature on reading and its implications for reading instruction* (NIH Pub. No. 00-4769).Washington, DC: NIHHD.

Nottingham, J., Nottingham, J., & Renton, M. (2017). *Challenging learning through dialogue: Strategies to engage your students and develop their language of learning*. Thousand Oaks, CA: Corwin Press.

Nystrand, M. (1997). *Opening dialogue*. New York: Teachers College Press.

Nystrand, M., Wu, L. L., Gamoran, A., Zeiser, S., & Long, D. A. (2003). Questions in time: Investigating the structure and dynamics of unfolding classroom discourse, *Discourse Processes*, *35*(2), 135–198.

Oakes, J., & Lipton, M. (1999). *Teaching to change the world*. New York: McGraw-Hill College.

O'Keefe, V. (1995). *Speaking to think; thinking to speak: The importance of talk in the learning process*. Portsmouth, NH: Boyton/Cook Publishers.

Ostroff, W. L. (2012). *Understanding how young children learn: Bringing the science of child development to the classroom.* Alexandria, VA: ASCD.

Ostroff, W. (2016). *Cultivating curiosity in K–12 classrooms*. Alexandria, VA: ASCD.

Partnership for 21st Century Learning. (2019). *Framework for 21st century learning*. Columbus, OH: Battelle for Kids.

Perkins D. (1992). *Smart schools: Better thinking and learning for every child*. New York: Free Press.

Perkins, D. (2014). *Future wise: Educating our children for a changing world*. San Francisco: Jossey Bass.

Postman, N., & Weingartner, C. (1969). *Teaching as a subversive activity*. New York, NY: Dell Publishing Company.

Proyas, A. (Director). (2004). *I robot*. Twentieth Century Fox; Mediastream Vierte Film GmbH & Co. Vermarktungs KG; Davis Entertainment; Laurence Mark Productions; Overbook Entertainment; Canlaws Productions.

Ritchhart, R. (2015). *Creating cultures of thinking: The 8 forces we must master to truly transform our schools*. San Francisco: Jossey-Bass.

Ritchhart, R. (2019). See-think-wonder. Cambridge MA: Project Zero, Harvard Graduate School of Education.

Ritchhart, R., & Church, M. (2020). The power of making thinking visible: Practices to engage and empower all learners. Hoboken, NJ: Jossey-Bass.

Ritchhart, R., Church, M., & Morrison, K. (2011). *Making thinking visible: How to promote engagement, understanding, and independence for all learners*. San Francisco: Jossey Bass.

Roberts, T., & Billings, L. (1999). *The Paideia Classroom: Teaching for understanding*. Larchmont, NY: Eye on Education.

Rothstein, D., & Santana, L. (2011). *Make just one change: Teach students to ask their own questions*. Cambridge, MA: Harvard Education Press.

Rowe, M. B. (1972). Wait time and rewards as instructional variables, their influence on language, logic, and fate control: Part one—Wait time. *Journal of Research in Science Teaching, 11*(2), 81–94.

Rowe, M. B. (1986). Slowing down may be a way of speeding up! *Journal of Teacher Education, 37*(1), 43–50.

Sadker, M., & Sadker, D. (1985). Is the OK classroom OK? *Phi Delta Kappan, 66*(5), 358–361.

Schlesinger, A. B. (2009). *The death of why?: The decline of questioning and the future of democracy*. San Francisco: Berrett-Koehler Publishers.

Strong, M. (1997). *The habit of thought: From Socratic seminars to Socratic practice*. Chapel Hill, NC: New View.

Tobin, K. (1987). The role of wait time in higher cognitive learning. *Review of Educational Research, 57*, 69–95.

Tucker, C. R. (2020). *Balance with blended learning: Partner with your students to reimagine learning and reclaim your life*. Thousand Oaks, CA: Corwin.

Turnbull, N. (2004). *What is the status of questioning in John Dewey's philosophy?* Paper presented to the Australasian Political Studies Association Conference, The University of Adelaide, September 29 through October, 2, 2004. https://tinyurl.com/ybdj4zyu

Wagner, T., & Dintersmith, T. (2015). *Most likely to succeed: Preparing our kids for the innovation era*. New York: Simon & Schuster.

Walsh, J. A., & Sattes, B. (2005). *Quality questioning: Research-based practice to engage every learner*. Thousand Oaks, CA: Corwin.

Walsh, J. A., & Sattes, B. (2011). *Thinking through quality questioning: Deepening student engagement*. Thousand Oaks, CA: Corwin.

Walsh, J. A., & Sattes, B. (2015a). A new rhythm for responding. *Educational Leadership, 73*(1), 46–52.

Walsh, J. A., & Sattes, B. (2015b). *Questioning for classroom discussion: Purposeful speaking, engaged listening, deep thinking*. Alexandria, VA: ASCD.

Walsh, J. A., & Sattes, B. (2017). *Quality questioning: Research-based practice to engage every learner* (2nd ed). Thousand Oaks, CA: Corwin.

Way, J. (2011). *Using questioning to stimulate mathematical thinking*. Cambridge, England: NRICH, University of Cambridge.

Wells, G. (2001). The case for dialogic inquiry. In G. Wells (Ed.), *Action, talk and text: Learning and teaching through inquiry* (pp. 171–294). New York: Teachers College Press.

Wiliam, D. (2011). *Embedded formative assessment*. Bloomington, IN: Solution Tree.

Index

Academic questions, 10, 16, 62, 126
    daily lessons, 70–71
    invite reflection, 73
    mindframes, 63–64
    model question-asking, think-alouds, 68
    practice with feedback, 72–73
    routines and protocols, 68–70
    strategies and skills, 64–68
    time and space, 71–72
Achievement gaps, 5–6
Adler, M., 113
Agency, 124
Alexander, R., 100, 104
Alvermann, D. E., 57
Anchor.fm, 96
Arguments, 5–6
Attitudes, 9, 21, 83, 117
Auditory displays, 95
Authentic question, 106

Barell, J., 84, 85
Barkley, M., 80 (box), 81, 82
Bath, P., 83
"Bell-ringer" activity, 48
Berger, R., 128
Berlyne, D., 82
Blogger, 52
Bohannon, K., 45, 85, 86 (box)
Breakout rooms, 95
Brown, A. L., 63

Campione, J. C., 63
Capacity building process, 27 (figure)
    academic questions, 63–73
    daily lessons, 29–30
    dialogic questions, 101–119
    exploratory questions, 82–93
    invite reflection, 31
    mindframes, 27–28

model question-asking, think-alouds, 28
    practice with feedback, 30–31
    routines and protocols, 29
    self-questioning, 52–57
    self-regulation, 39–52
    strategies and stems, 28
    time and space, 30
Carver, G. W., 83
Celebrate It principle, 22
Chalk Talk, 46
Child, D. A., 39
Chin, C., 57
Church, M., 2
City, E., 114 (box)
Civic responsibility, 4
Clark, A., 64, 69, 70, 76, 96
ClassDojo, 51, 59, 121
Classroom(s)
    behaviors, 10
    conversations, 105–106
    cultures, 20–22, 81
    daily routines, 47, 70
    data collection, strategies, 73
    pacing, 71–72
    research, 6–7
    "right-answer" oriented, 11
    scaffolding, 125–128
    science, 57
    seminars, 113–114
    social studies, 55–56
    student perceptions and behaviors, 20
    student-to-student questioning, 108
    talk, 11, 101
    teacher-centered, 62
    time and space issue, 30
    traditional, 14, 20, 63
Copeland, M., 114 (box)
Costa, A., 127
COVID-19 pandemic, 124

Curie, M., 83
Curiosity, 4, 10, 16, 22, 38, 67
    activation of, 81
    attitudes and beliefs, 83
    celebrations, 93
    cultivation of, 80
    daily lessons, 90–91
    expression of, 28, 81, 86, 92
    innate, 22, 23
    instinctive, 22
    knowledge gaps, 81
    pique, 87
    types, 82
Curiosity walks, 89
Cycle of Student Self-Questioning to Learn,
    40–43, 41 (figure)

Data collection, 73
Dawes, L., 106
Deep learning, 4, 57, 64, 66, 81, 116
Dewey, J., 4, 20
Dialogic questions, 10, 16, 126, 127
    crafting, 105
    daily lessons, 114–116
    defined, 100–101
    invite reflection, 117–119
    listening, 102–103
    mindframes, 101–102
    model question-asking, think-alouds,
        105–108
    online opportunities, 120–121
    practice with feedback, 116–117
    purposes, 104, 104 (box)
    routines and protocols, 108–114
    sample prompt and stems, 102, 103 (figure)
    time and space, 116
Dillon, J. T., 3, 7, 24, 27, 101, 116
Dintersmith, T., 3
DOK 1 levels, 28
Donoghue, G., 7, 58

Edison, T., 83
Educational leaders, responsibility of, 4
Einstein, 83
Engel, S., 80, 82, 87, 90, 94
Enthusiasm, 81, 93
Epistemic curiosity, 82
Exploratory questions, 10, 16, 126
    criteria for, 92, 92 (figure)
    daily lessons, 90–91
    defined, 80, 82

invite reflection, 93
mindframe, 83–84
model question-asking, think-alouds, 84–86
online opportunities, 95–96
practice with feedback, 92–93
routines and protocols, 86–90
skills and strategies, 84, 85 (figure)
time and space, 91

Fishbowl, 116
Flipgrid, 59, 75, 95, 96, 121
Four A's text protocol, 109, 110 (box)
Fullan, M., 4, 81

Goodwin, B., 80, 82
Goodwin, J., 5 (box)
Google Classroom, 75
Google Docs, 52
Google Meet, 59, 75, 121
Google Sites, 52

Hale, M., 114 (box)
Haller, E. P., 39
Hand-raising, 14
Hattie, J., 7, 39, 58, 64, 76, 100, 102, 127–128
Hendrix, S., 89 (box)
Herschel, C., 83

Imagine It principle, 21
Informal Inventory of Student Question-
    Asking, 24, 25 (figure), 26 (figure)
Initiate-Respond-Evaluate (IRE) model, 11, 90
Ink Think, 46–47
Innate curiosity, 22–23
Insight—Question (IQ) Pairs, 68, 69, 75
Instinctive curiosity, 22
Intentional instruction, 22–24
Interruptions, 6
Interview Design protocol, 7, 111,
    111–112 (box), 113
IRE model. *See* Initiate-Respond-Evaluate
    (IRE) model

Jamboard, 76, 95, 96
Joyous exploration, 93 (box)

Kaizena, 76
Kallick, B., 127
Knowledge gaps, 81
Know-Want to Know-Learned (KWL)
    template, 46

Learning management system (LMS), 75, 96
Leonardo, 83
Leslie, I., 90
Levy, F., 129
LMS. *See* Learning management system (LMS)

MacKenzie, T., 89, 90
Making Thinking Visible (Ritchhart, Church, & Morrison), 87
Mathematical problem-solving, 56, 56 (figure)
McCann, T. M., 115
Mentimeter, 76
Mercer, N., 106
Microsoft Teams, 75, 95
Mindframes, 9–10, 20, 31, 33, 129
    academic questions, 63–64, 74, 75
    concept of, 127
    dialogic questions, 101–102, 120
    exploratory questions, 83–84, 93, 95
    focus on, 27–28
    self-questioning, 52, 59
    self-regulation, 40, 51
    student adoption, 128
Mintz, K., 105 (box), 124 (box)
Moore, J., 5, 6, 62, 115, 116
Murnane, R. J., 129

National Paideia Center, 113
National Reading Panel, 53
National School Reform Faculty, 46
Nystrand, M., 106

O'Keefe, V., 23
Online opportunities
    academic questions, 75–76
    dialogic questions, 120–121
    exploratory questions, 95–96
    meaning-making questions, 59
    self-regulation questions, 51–52
    student questions, 33–34
Own It principle, 22

Padlet, 76, 95, 96
Paideia Proposal, The (Adler), 113
Passion, 81, 84
Patterson, J., 55 (box)
Pear Deck, 76, 96
Peer feedback, 67, 72, 116
Perceptual curiosity, 82
Phifer, L., 100 (box)
Picasso, 83

Pinkard, B., 23 (box)
Power of Making Thinking Visible, The (Ritchhart & Church), 87
Praise-Question-Polish (PQP), 72, 73
Project Zero, 46, 69, 70

Quality questions
    developing and assessing, 67–68
    dialogic, 105, 111
    features and functions, 11
Questioning Circle, 87, 87–88 (box), 95
Questioning culture
    features/functions of quality, 11
    students voice, 14–15
    teaching practices and environmental factors, 10
    think times, 11–14
Questioning for Classroom Discussion (Walsh & Sattes), 102
Question types, 125–127, 125 (figure)
    developing knowledge of, 8–9

Ray, T., 20, 21, 31 (box), 49 (box), 50, 76, 83, 96
Reading comprehension, 53–55
Reflective questioning, 117, 118–119 (box), 119
Reproductive performance, 64
Revised Bloom Remember levels, 28
Right Question Institute, 68
Ritchhart, R., 2, 46, 87, 108, 109
Roosegaarde, D., 81
Round-Robin Questioning, 70, 71, 75
Rowe, M. B., 6, 11

Sattes, B., 7, 102
Scaffolding, 12, 15, 16, 22, 23 (box), 29, 31, 40, 42, 46, 51, 55 (box), 58, 59, 68, 69, 70 (box), 72 (box), 81, 84, 92, 95, 102, 108–110, 113 (box), 116, 120, 125–128
Schlesinger, A. B., 4
Schoology, 75
Scientific thinking, 57–58
Screencastify, 96
SeeSaw, 51, 59, 95, 96, 121
See-Think-Wonder, 55 (box), 69, 87, 95
Self-assessment, 72, 92, 116
Self-efficacy, 9
Self-questioning, 10, 16
    mathematical problem-solving, 56, 56 (figure)
    meaning-making, 39, 52–59
    metacognitive approach, importance of, 38
    reading comprehension strategies, 53–55

scientific thinking, 57–58
self-regulation, 39–52
social studies classrooms, 55–56
Self-regulation questions, 39
   daily lessons, 47–48
   description, 58
   invite reflection, 48–50
   model question-asking, think-alouds, 44–45
   online opportunities, 51–52
   practice with feedback, 48
   routines and protocols, 45–47
   skills, 43–44, 44 (figure)
   strategy, 40–43
   time and space, 48
Seminars, 113–114, 114 (box)
Shelton, M., 2, 6, 100 (box), 113, 113 (box)
Smith, W., 564
Social injustice, 100 (box), 113 (box)
Social studies classrooms, 55–56
Socratic circles and seminars, 113–114,
   114 (box)
Somers, C., 72
Spotlight It principle, 22
State curiosity, 82
Structure It principle, 22
Student empowerment, 16
Student questions
   arguments, 5–6
   categories, 5
   online opportunities, 33–34
   ownership of learning, 2–4
   school leaders, 4
   skill, will, and *thrill,* 7–15
   strategies and structures, 15
Surface learning, 64, 65

Talk&Comment, 76
Target students, 14

Taxonomy of Student Questions, 8–9,
   9 (figure), 126
Teacher-centered classrooms, 62
Teachers as activators, 15, 125
   capacity building process, 24, 27–31,
      27 (figure)
   classroom culture, 20–22
   Informal Inventory of Student Question-
      Asking, 24, 25 (figure), 26 (figure)
   intentional instruction, 22–24
   modeling, 44, 106–107
   reflection, 39 (box)
Think-alouds, 28, 44–45, 47, 53, 55, 68, 84–86,
   105–108
Think-Pair-Share (TPS), 110–113
Think-Puzzle-Explore (TPE), 46, 51, 69, 87
Think times, 11–13, 12 (figure), 30
To Kill A Mockingbird, 2
Trait curiosity, 82
Transfer learning, 66–67
Tucker, C. R., 52

Virtual learning, 17
Visual displays, 95
Vocaroo, 76
VoiceThread, 76
Voxer, 76

Wagner, T., 3
Walberg, H. J., 39
Way, J., 56
Whaley, J., 13 (box)
Wonderment questions, 57–58
Woodrow, L., 13 (box)

Young, B., 105 (box), 124 (box)

Zoom, 51, 59, 75, 95, 96, 121

A SAGE Publishing Company

Helping educators make the greatest impact

CORWIN HAS ONE MISSION: to enhance education through intentional professional learning.

We build long-term relationships with our authors, educators, clients, and associations who partner with us to develop and continuously improve the best evidence-based practices that establish and support lifelong learning.

Solutions YOU WANT | Experts YOU TRUST | Results YOU NEED

EVENTS

>>> INSTITUTES

Corwin Institutes provide large regional events where educators collaborate with peers and learn from industry experts. Prepare to be recharged and motivated!

corwin.com/institutes

ON-SITE PD

>>> ON-SITE PROFESSIONAL LEARNING

Corwin on-site PD is delivered through high-energy keynotes, practical workshops, and custom coaching services designed to support knowledge development and implementation.

corwin.com/pd

>>> PROFESSIONAL DEVELOPMENT RESOURCE CENTER

The PD Resource Center provides school and district PD facilitators with the tools and resources needed to deliver effective PD.

corwin.com/pdrc

ONLINE

>>> ADVANCE

Designed for K–12 teachers, Advance offers a range of online learning options that can qualify for graduate-level credit and apply toward license renewal.

corwin.com/advance

Contact a PD Advisor at (800) 831-6640 or visit www.corwin.com for more information